WITH BANDS OF LOVE

Lessons from the Book of Hosea

by

DAVID ALLAN HUBBARD
President, Fuller Theological Seminary

William B. Eerdmans P~~~~~~~ ~~~~~~~
Grand Rapids,

WITH BANDS OF LOVE

Lessons from the Book of Hosea

PREFACE

The contents of this little book were originally given as Sunday School lessons to the Mariners Class of the Lake Avenue Congregational Church of Pasadena, California. Some of the materials have been adapted from four lectures on Hosea given at the Conservative Baptist Seminary in Denver, Colorado.

It goes without saying that this is not a commentary on the prophecy of Hosea but rather some theological observations which stem from his preaching. I have attempted to understand the prophet's message in its own setting and at the same time to intimate the ways in which his oracles anticipate the fuller revelation of God in the New Testament and impinge on contemporary life and thought.

Anyone who writes a popular work on Hosea is deeply obligated to the scholarly efforts of predecessors too numerous to mention. It would be unfair, however, for me to fail to acknowledge my indebtedness to Professor H. H. Rowley, whose essay on "The Marriage of Hosea" originally appeared in the *Bulletin of the John Rylands Library*, XXXIX (1956-57) and has been reprinted in *Men of God* (London: Thomas Nelson and Sons, 1963). Biblical quotations are from the Revised Standard Version of the Bible, Old Testament Section, Copyright 1952, by Division of Christian Education of the National Council of the Churches of Christ in the United States of America.

The tedious task of translating these chapters from oral to written form has been accomplished largely by my friend Mary Claire Gautschi.

To my wife, Ruth, goes credit for the final typing of the manuscript.

CONTENTS

When Israel was a child, I loved him,
    and out of Egypt I called my son.
The more I called them,
    the more they went from me.

    . . . . .
I led them with cords of compassion,
    with the bands of love.
               (Hosea 11:1, 4)

INTRODUCTION

Hosea, like all the prophets, spoke within the cultural, political, social, and religious context of his time. He was a voice of God crying in the wilderness of Israel's degradation, and in his tragic marriage he dramatically demonstrated God's redemptive love for man. Although his book reveals his sharp awareness of the past and a rare ability to envision Israel's future with the eyes of God, it was the incendiary issues of the day that sparked his ministry to flame.

Hosea's marriage and his message are the two main themes, which interweave with the two strands of God's judgment and God's grace to form the pattern of his writing. This poignant story of one-sided love relates Hosea's obedience to God's command to take Gomer as his wife, Gomer's desertion of her husband, and her subsequent reconciliation to Hosea.

This relationship is the heart of Hosea's message. Symbolized in his marriage to Gomer and made explicit in the new marriage between God and Israel in chapters two and three, it dominates the first part of the book. Here the prophet looks beyond the present waywardness of his people and sees a future engagement — an eternal betrothal — in which God's faithfulness is matched by Israel's devotion and a new and lasting relationship is brought about (2:14-23; 3:5).

Throughout most of the latter part of the book (chapters four to fourteen) the corruption and futility of the Israelites' deteriorating relationship with God contrast shockingly with the ideal covenant relationship pictured earlier. In the midst of the alternating themes of wrath toward sin and mercy in spite of it, the prophet takes great pains to spell out the iniquities that shaped the doom of the old relationship and the complete change of direction that must characterize the new.

Rarely has a person been better equipped by way of talents, training, calling, and experience to proclaim God's truth in his generation. Rarely has any man used such equipment so worthily in the service of God. The wholehearted response of the people of God through the ages to Hosea's message is ample testimony to its quality, authority, and inspiration.

As Hosea penetrates the facades of idolatrous Israel, revealing the holiness of God and proclaiming the nature of true religious experience, his book becomes an exposé of the sinful condition of men of all times. It is a diagnosis of the chronic sickness of the human soul and a timeless prescription of love and grace as the remedy.

Chapter One

THE MAN BEHIND THE MESSAGE

When the Lord first spoke through Hosea,
the Lord said to Hosea. . . .
(Hosea 1:2)

How would a man like Hosea have fared in our day?

In a society where the public image is the thing, and the woman behind the man is thought to hold the key to his success, what would have been the fate of this upright citizen who suddenly married, of all people, a prostitute?

In a generation that regards self-expression and self-fulfillment as the goals toward which the well-adjusted strive, how would this single-purposed man who relentlessly pursued the goal of obedience to God have been received?

In a world that practices a kind of moral disarmament and assumes that truth, if it is to be spoken at all, must be diluted, sugared, and given in small doses, what would have been the response to this forthright man of God?

The fact is that Hosea would not have been given a high rating on the Gallup Poll of any age; for, as Scripture points out, the heart of man is desperately corrupt. The case of the Israelites, who had turned from God and righteous living, is not so unusual. The unusualness lies in the character and degree of personal commitment of the man God called to be his harbinger of judgment and grace.

It will be the purpose of this chapter to bring the prophet Hosea into clearer focus by discussing his occupation, his personal qualities, the characteristics of his writing, and the nature of his call.

God's message, because it comes from the heart of a personal God and is directed to the needs of human personalities, has always been conveyed through persons. It has been God's practice from the beginning to establish a personal relationship with all men by speaking first *to* a chosen few and then speaking *through* them.

These divinely appointed spokesmen were far more than mere puppets whose every word and action would be regulated from above. Their phrasings, figures of speech, and emphases were their own, and their individual personalities, cultural backgrounds, and talents were used in this revelatory process.

Isaiah's familiarity with national and international politics and his close acquaintance with the court life and protocol revealed themselves in his message. Contrast him, for instance, with Micah, the prophet of the poor, the peasant farmer from the hill country in southern Judah. It is no accident that Ezekiel, who came from a priestly family, took a keen interest in the formal religious life of Israel and described the future in terms of a new temple and a pure worship.

Each prophet was a personality so charged by the Spirit of God that what the man was saying, God was saying.

This helps to account for the fact that in almost all of the prophetic books there are sudden switches from the voice of the prophet to the voice of God, or the other way around.

Hosea is not mentioned in any other book in the Old Testament. Nothing is known about him except what can be gleaned from his fourteen chapters by examining his direct statements and by reading between the lines.

One of the lessons to be learned from this lack of information is that the prophet's message is more important than the prophet's personal background or the prophet's personality. The prophet himself stands in the wings while his message takes the center stage, not because the prophet himself is unimportant, but because it is his message that is central.

Hosea's Occupation

There has been a great deal of speculation among Biblical scholars as to the occupation of Hosea. Was he trained to be a prophet, schooled in a prophetic guild as one of the "sons of the prophets"? Or did he, like Amos, have a trade which he left temporarily to carry on his prophetic activity? At least four suggestions have been made as to his background.

His preoccupation with the corruption of the priesthood has suggested to some that he was raised in this office and was gripped by the failure of his colleagues to discharge their responsibilities. Of the priests he says,

> They feed on the sin of my people;
>> they are greedy for their iniquity.
> And it shall be like people, like priest;
>> I will punish them for their ways,

> and requite them for their deeds.
>> (4:8, 9)

"Like people, like priest." As the priests shared in the people's corruption by encouraging false worship and flagrant disregard of the law (which they should have been teaching and upholding), so they would share in judgment for their disobedience. The priests were especially blameworthy because the patriarchal social and political system made the commoners strongly dependent upon these established leaders.

It is probably going beyond the evidence to brand Hosea as a priest. It may be that he, like several other prophets, was concerned with the priests as he was concerned with all the leaders of Israel, and that he spoke to them directly and definitely not because he was one of their members trying to bring them into line, but because he was a conscientious Israelite who realized the corruption of the priesthood:

> Hear this, O priests!
>> Give heed, O house of Israel!
> Hearken, O house of the king!
>> For the judgment pertains to you;
> for you have been a snare at Mizpah,
>> and a net spread upon Tabor.
>>> (5:1)

Another point of view sees Hosea as a professional prophet especially trained for his ministry. His mention of a definite call in 1:2 seems to argue against this. The fact that he flays the false prophets along with the corrupt priests (4:5) may well indicate that he did not choose to associate himself with them. At the same time, he supports the ministry of the true prophets who were subject to continual abuse at the hands of a calloused people.

The days of punishment have come,
the days of recompense have come;
Israel shall know it.
The prophet is a fool,
the man of the spirit is mad,
because of your great iniquity
and great hatred.
The prophet is the watchman of Ephraim,
the people of my God,
yet a fowler's snare is on all his ways,
and hatred in the house of his God.
(9:7, 8)

God had sent prophets as watchmen, charged with warning the people of danger. In response, the rebellious people were treating the prophets with contempt by labeling them fools and madmen.

So we cannot say with any certainty that Hosea was either priest or professional prophet. We can only say that, in common with his great colleagues, he took a serious and personal interest in the prevalent abuse of these offices.

Some have tried to get at the problem of Hosea's background through his literary style and his figures of speech. In chapter seven, for instance, he gives an extended metaphor comparing the hot intrigue of Samaria's noblemen to a baker's oven. The suggestion has been made on the basis of this that Hosea himself may have been a baker by trade. However, baking in antiquity was not an esoteric process, and there is little need to feel that Hosea must have been an insider in order to have described in detail how the baker went about his daily routine.

Another suggestion based on his literary style and figures of speech would view him as a farmer. In some ways this is the most attractive suggestion because by and large his metaphors are rural:

> For they sow the wind,
> and they shall reap the whirlwind.
> The standing grain has no heads,
> it shall yield no meal;
> if it were to yield,
> aliens would devour it.
>
> (8:7)

Again,

> You have plowed iniquity,
> you have reaped injustice,
> you have eaten the fruit of lies. . . .
> (10:13)

Although there are many agricultural metaphors to be found in Hosea, caution is necessary here because the northern kingdom was an agricultural kingdom and the Israelites in general were agricultural people. But there is sufficient emphasis on rural life to suggest that Hosea, like Micah in the south, may well have been a man of the soil.

Hosea's Character

Hosea was probably an uncommon person even before God asked him to undergo the uncommon experience that his book relates. His rare combination of traits, attitudes, and insights is paralleled in the Old Testament only in the person of Jeremiah.

His tenderness and compassion mark him off from sterner men like Amos and Isaiah. As few men before or after, he had passed through the refining fires of personal suffering and emerged free from the dross of bitterness and resentment which have clouded many a lesser soul. His compassion for his people and his understanding of God's heartbreak and disappointment are apparent on almost every page.

Many of Hosea's most profound passages do not seem to record public utterances, but rather give voice to the kind of reflections that would be made in solitude or perhaps in the company of a handful of disciples as he meditated on his people's plight. Contrast, for instance, the bold warnings of 5:1ff. with the somber musings of 10:1-8. We have no indication that Hosea shied away from the market place, but we do have evidence that some of his prophesying took place in private. Reflections like those in 8:11-13, expressed in the third person, bear witness to a contemplative, pensive trait within the prophet.

This is not to say that he could not flash forth in ire when occasion demanded. The biting quality of some of his metaphors—"Ephraim is like a dove, silly and without sense" (7:11) or "Like a stubborn heifer, Israel is stubborn" (4:16)—and the stinging indictments of sin and corruption are ample evidences of his courage and forthrightness. He was sensitive to sin and unrighteousness as one who knew intimately the hurt of such conduct, and he spared no effort in placarding the destructive effects of irresponsible actions.

Though the religious life of his people was his main concern, he did not ignore their political situation. It is well for us who are used to rigid distinctions between Church and State to remember that the Old Testament made no such distinction. Israel's king was her religious as well as her political leader, and his political decisions had deep religious significance as they affected the actions and attitudes

of the people. Hosea was alert to the political tensions within
Israel and throughout the Middle East, as his frequent ref-
erences to Assyria and Egypt indicate (7:11; 9:3; 11:5;
12:1, etc.). Because he was well aware of the political
ambivalence of the Israelites who vacillated between Assyria
and Egypt in trying to determine on whom they should
depend, Hosea's constant call was to reliance upon and
loyalty to the God of the covenant, who alone was to be
their shield and stay.

Each prophet is an individual, endowed by God with
distinct gifts, placed by God in a specific setting, and called
by God to a unique ministry. Hosea's traits of character,
personal experiences, and methods of presenting his message
are his own and mark him off from the other prophets. He
was inspired by the Spirit of God, sensitive to the Word
of God, yielding to the will of God; but most important,
he was himself; and that is exactly what God wanted him
to be.

Hosea's Literary Skill

Though Hosea may well have come from a rural background, he was far from being an uninformed peasant. Few
poets in the Old Testament write with more skill and
beauty than he. His figures of speech are both clear and
striking. Can you think of a better way to describe the
instability and uncertainty of Israel's foreign policy than
this?

> Ephraim is like a dove,
>   silly and without sense,
>   calling to Egypt, going to Assyria.
>   (7:11)

Or how better depict the futility of trusting in human resources than this?

> Ephraim herds the wind,
>> and pursues the east wind all day long. . . .
>> (12:1)

The prose passages in chapters one and three are prize examples of the simple profoundness which the best Hebrew writers display:

> When the Lord first spoke through Hosea, the Lord said to Hosea, "Go, take to yourself a wife of harlotry and have children of harlotry, for the land commits great harlotry by forsaking the Lord." So he went and took Gomer the daughter of Diblaim, and she conceived and bore him a son.
>> (1:2, 3)

The power of the tragedy lies starkly before us in the simplicity of the prose.

Hosea's skill as a writer shows itself also in the variety of tone and structure to be found in his oracles. Sometimes he uses the language of the law court as he calls out his stern indictments like a judge:

> Hear the word of the Lord, O people of Israel;
>> for the Lord has a controversy with the
>> inhabitants of the land;
> There is no faithfulness or kindness,
>> and no knowledge of God in the land.
>> (4:1)

At other times he uses the language of the military commanders as they would bark out their orders when threatened by aggressors:

> Blow the horn in Gibeah,
>> the trumpet in Ramah.

>   Sound the alarm at Beth-aven;
>   tremble, O Benjamin!
>   (5:8)

Just as the prophetic oracles were not revealed in a
historical vacuum but reflect the tensions of the times, so
they are not declared in a literary vacuum but are based
on literary forms and types well known in the ancient East,
and particularly Israel. We will understand more of their
impact and appreciate more fully the content and mood
they convey when we realize they are phrased in terms
or structured in techniques that had intellectual and emo-
tional meaning to their hearers.

It is in lyric power and pathos that Hosea's real genius
lies. His ability to convey the anguish within the heart of
a God rejected by his people is unparalleled. If he does not
match the strong cadences of Amos, who cries, "But let
justice roll down like waters, and righteousness like an ever-
flowing stream" (Amos 5:24), and if his writing does not
rival the careful literary strains and polished stylizing of the
herdsman from Tekoa, there is a beauty and a depth of
feeling that Amos only rarely approached:

>   Therefore, behold, I will allure her,
>   and bring her into the wilderness,
>   and speak tenderly to her.
>   And there I will give her her vineyards,
>   and make the valley of Achor a door of hope.
>   And there she shall answer as in the days of her youth,
>   as at the time when she came out of the
>   land of Egypt.
>   (2:14, 15)

Hosea's lyric style shines through his writings in many
passages. Good examples are 9:10; 11:1-9; 14:7.

In Hosea's writing we find a commendable blend of message and style. Neither outshines the other. Spirit and form are so beautifully wed that what he says is made memorable by the way he says it. We can learn from him and the other Biblical writers the importance of expressing the Christian message in a manner worthy of it. It is fitting that we avoid elaborate embellishments and high-flown oratory, but it is vital that we resist the temptation to clothe priceless truths in tattered clichés.

Clarity, beauty, and power are the attributes of a gifted writer. We find them combined in Hosea. His crucial message was given a timeless setting because of these gifts. He is an example to all men of faith to strive for ways to make graphic the Good News and to use all possible skill in demonstrating the ways in which God, through Christ, has given final answer to man's nagging questions.

Hosea's Prophetic Ministry

We are not told how and when Hosea was called to be a prophet. It is possible that the command to marry (1:2) was itself the call, though Hosea may not have realized it until afterward. It is more likely that his call preceded the marriage and was intensified by it. In any case it is clear that by the time the first child was born Hosea was fulfilling his role as a prophet, because he named his son Jezreel at the command of God.

That Hosea had a direct and compelling divine summons to prophesy we cannot doubt, even though the details are not given. Only the conviction that he was fulfilling a holy commission would have enabled him to face his tragic circumstances with unrelenting courage and loyalty.

Prophetic calls in Scripture take many forms, as the experiences of Abraham, Moses, Samuel, Amos, Isaiah, Jeremiah, Ezekiel, and Paul indicate. But one thing that all of them had in common was a sense of inescapable obligation to carry out the will of God. In the main, they were not professional prophets, born and raised to their responsibilities. They did not perform their duties as a means of gaining a livelihood. They were under a divine compulsion which drove them to act when they would have chosen to shy away from involvement; to speak when they preferred to keep silent; to suffer persecution when they longed for acceptance and approval. Hosea's life and message eminently qualified him to join their ranks.

The false prophets or mere professionals tailored their messages to suit the whims of the people. Hosea did not. False prophets skirted the real issues of sin and judgment. Hosea could not. False prophets were stained with the dye of the people's rebellion and disobedience. Hosea was not. His call, and especially the lessons learned from his tragic marriage, marked him off from the false prophets of his day and gave him an uncommon understanding of God's ways and a fearless authority to proclaim them.

The insistence of prophets like Hosea that what they were preaching was indeed the Word of God may seem puzzling to us. Just how did God speak? How did the Word of the Lord come to the prophet? The Bible suggests a number of ways. Sometimes God spoke through extraordinary visions, like the picture of the living creatures and wheels in Ezekiel 1:4ff. At other times God inspired the prophet to find a special meaning in some natural object or everyday occurrence, as in the case of Amos's visions of the plumbline and the basket of summer fruit (Amos 7:7-9; 8:1-3). The Word of God came to Joel as he pondered the meaning of a ravaging plague of insects, and Nahum heard God's voice as he reflected on the downfall of Assyria and her proud capital, Nineveh.

God spoke to Hosea through his personal experiences with Gomer and her children. Apparently, as the prophet reflected on the infidelity of his wife, God made clear to him the deeper lessons of Israel's unfaithfulness. In seeing Israel's covenant relationship to God as a marriage contract, Hosea was given the perspective by which to judge the defection of his people and the pain it brought to the heart of God.

There is no evidence that visions contributed to Hosea's message. It is always hazardous to analyze spiritual experience, but it seems likely that God spoke to Hosea within his own consciousness. Perhaps great convictions and even the actual phrases would come to his mind as he considered his own situation and that of his countrymen. He knew intuitively that God was impelling him to speak and implanting the message within him. He must have felt constrained to say things that he would not have chosen to say without this divine urging. He needed no set occasion or formal invitation. As another prophet put it: "The Lord God has spoken; who can but prophesy?" (Amos 3:8).

We look in vain throughout his writings for a hint of rebellion against or even indifference toward the divine mandate. The command to marry Gomer is obeyed with dispatch and without discussion (1:2-3). The names of the children are given by heavenly command. The even sterner order to remarry Gomer despite her wantonness is duly car-

ried out by the prophet. The book is devoid of any evidence
that there is within the prophet the kind of struggling and
wrestling that Jeremiah openly relates. But who can doubt
that Hosea felt the hurt and humiliation of this costly kind
of discipleship?

Hosea spoke of the future, but he was not primarily a
predictor. Nor was any of the prophets. They applied the
insights of the past and the hope of the future to the needs
of the present. Their "predictions" did not come out of
the blue, but were based on their analysis of political and
sociological factors, and of the moral quality of the people.
Often what may appear to be absolute predictions are rather
conditional warnings — what surely will occur *unless* the people change in some way (cf. Jeremiah 18:7ff.).

Their chief role was to interpret the meaning of the
covenant for their times. They pressed the demands of that
great transaction upon Israel and interpreted her history
in the light of her obedience or disobedience to this basic
relationship. It was this message that Hosea, as one of the
great prophets, heralded — a message of God's faithfulness
in wrath and grace, a message rooted in Israel's past, relevant
to Israel's present, and moving to fulfillment in Israel's
future.

Chapter Two

THE TIMES THAT SHAPED THE MESSAGE: THREAT FROM WITHOUT

Ephraim is like a dove,
      silly and without sense,
      calling to Egypt, going to Assyria.
                              (Hosea 7:11)

It is a truism to say that God speaks within the framework of history rather than apart from it. His message is not something that is packaged and handed down in a signed-sealed-and-delivered fashion; it is vitally involved in the circumstances of the times. It is God breaking into our human experiences and letting us know what he is like and what we are like. It is God shedding light on the human predicament and disclosing the divine solution to that predicament; not merely in our moments of retreat or detachment, but in the midst of the busy press of life.

God chose the prophets as interpreters of his work in Israel's history. As such, the prophets were neither blind predictors nor mystic visionaries who in telescopic fashion peered down through the centuries and focused on what was going to happen. When Biblical prediction does have this telescopic quality it is, in reality, the prophet's understanding of the nature of a God who has guided in times past and present and will bring his program to fulfillment in the future. There is a direct relationship between what the prophet says about Israel's history, what he says about the present (the moment of crisis, of trial, of confusion, to which he is addressing himself), and what he says about the future.

Predictions that deal with the future alone do the present little good. It does not really help those in present distress to know that in five hundred years God is going to work everything out all right. The question is, "What is he doing now?" What the prophet is saying is that God is acting both now and in the future, and there is a continuity in his activity. What he is doing today is related to what he will do tomorrow. The future is seen not as something floating out in the great beyond, but as the culmination of the program God has already begun in the past and is carrying on in the prophet's own time.

The most crucial period in Hosea's ministry spanned the years between 750 and 725 bc. Undoubtedly he began to prophesy before this time, as the reference in 1:1 to Jeroboam II (c. 792-753 bc) indicates; and the mention of Hezekiah (c. 715-686 bc) suggests that he carried on his ministry beyond 725 bc. But the heart of his message was proclaimed during this quarter century.

Some may be puzzled over the question of dating Old Testament events and writings. How can we be sure of dates like these? In the main, we are indebted to the Assyrians, who were meticulous date keepers. They named every year in their calendar after a key leader, so that every year had its own name. Furthermore, every period is distinguished in Assyrian records by some great event that took place. Perhaps their greatest contribution was the recording of unusual astronomical phenomena.

For instance, there was an eclipse of the sun in 763 BC. By astronomical calculations, it is possible to plot exactly when that eclipse took place and synchronize it with the Assyrian record. Once a fixed date is established, it can be dovetailed with the dates of Israel and a chronological pattern emerges.

Hosea's active ministry came to a close around 725. Israel fell in 721 or 722 when its capital city of Samaria was finally destroyed by the Assyrians. Although Hosea saw destruction coming, he left no record of the event itself in his writings.

There were two other key people, Micah and Isaiah, prophesying at the same time. Amos had come and gone by this time, blazing a trail of prophetic glory in Israel. Hosea took his place, preaching the Word of God in the north, in Samaria, while Micah and Isaiah were doing the same in the south, in and around Jerusalem. When it seemed as though sin had taken an almost inestimable toll, God sent his servants, the prophets, and brought light through his Word.

There are two points that should be brought into focus as we look at Hosea's times. The first is that he spoke silhouetted against the twilight of the splendid era of Jeroboam II. The other is that he spoke at the time when the neighboring Assyrians were coming into a new heyday of political strength.

The Close of Jeroboam's Reign

When the people of Israel came out of Egypt in the Exodus and settled in the land during the period of judges, "there was no king in Israel; every man did what was right in his own eyes" (Judges 17:6). The tribes were living disjointedly and separately; the only glue that held them together was their common faith in God, and the tabernacle to which they would come for worship during their seasonal festivities. There was no strong central government, no senate, no congress, no way of bringing about a fusion of national interests.

The only real leaders in this loose system of government were the independently operating, ever changing judges — hero figures whose responsibilities were political, judicial, military, and religious. Crisis, leadership arising in times of difficulty and then fading into oblivion as the difficulty eased, and then another judge arriving on the scene, performing his many-faceted role and exiting, to be replaced by another judge — such was the political pattern until the time of monarchy.

Under Saul and Samuel the monarchy was established because the Philistines were putting constant pressure on these scattered tribes, and the people of Israel knew that they could not continue their loose-knit organization and thrive. They knew that they needed a centralized government and more forceful leadership in order to resist the militant Philistines. The Israelites at that time had only bronze, and weapons of bronze could not cope with the iron weapons of the Philistines.

And so the monarchy arose, and after Saul came the establishment of the Davidic dynasty. David and his son

Solomon gave the Israelites their first taste of national glory. But it was short-lived and did not survive Solomon by long, because the basic loyalty of the people was to their own tribes, not to the central government.

After the loss of the iron-fisted leadership of David and Solomon, the cohesive element was gone and the kingdom split apart. Rehoboam, Solomon's son, was leader of the southern kingdom of Judah with its capital in Jerusalem. The northern kingdom of Israel was under Jeroboam I, an aggressive, nationalistic leader.

For almost two centuries following this division and throughout Hosea's ministry, there were two political entities — two separate kingdoms. In Hosea's time "Israel" (whose capital was in Samaria) referred to the northern kingdom of which he was a loyal member. The ruling monarch of that day was Jeroboam II, who is considered the greatest king of Israel.

Jeroboam brought to this northern kingdom a kind of Solomonic age by using many of the techniques that Solomon had used. He was a shrewd trader. He took advantage of the fact that the kingdom of Israel sat athwart the caravan lines between Syria, Assyria, Asia Minor, South Arabia, and Egypt, by collecting duties and taxes from the caravan trade. He had merchant ships which plied the waters of the Mediterranean, and profited from their cargoes. From these sources and others, wealth was flowing into the kingdom of Israel.

At the same time, Jeroboam's wealth enabled him to maintain a lavish military enterprise; so he began to chip away at some of the regions that David and Solomon had once controlled, such as the territory around Damascus and the northern part of Syria. He extended his power across

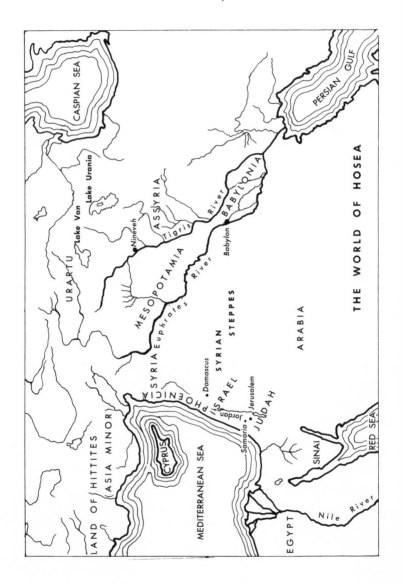

the Jordan to the lands of Gilead, Ammon, and Moab and was able to build for himself a substantial empire.

While Jeroboam's territorial acquisitions were building up, the covenant pattern within Israel was breaking down. The entire social and legal structure of Israel had been based upon a strong clan life with close family ties. The more commercial the society became, the more the clan structure deteriorated. An ever increasing number were going off to the cities to try to make their fortunes with Shylock-type merchants who knew how to buy low and sell high.

The crafty commercial practices for which the Canaanites were famous were now being employed by the Israelites. Sharp, cruel dealings were the order of the day. Exorbitant rates of interest were charged; mortgages of widows and orphans were foreclosed. Those who could no longer hold their own in private enterprise because they had lost all of their assets were forced to go into slavery; they could not make a living by normal means.

The prophet Amos tells about rich women in the city of Samaria whom he graphically describes as "the cows of Bashan." Well fed, affluent, living in luxury, they were continually badgering their husbands to make more money so that they could live in even greater luxury (Amos 4:1ff.). Oppression of the poor and corruption in the courts made this opulence possible.

This complete disregard of justice and social responsibility, principles that had been integral parts of Israelite society, caused the prophets to speak out in urgent voice. They deplored this anti-Israel way of life which did not involve a direct dependence upon God and which tore families asunder.

"How are we going to keep them down on the farm after they've seen Samaria?" became a burning question in the hearts and minds of prophets like Amos and Micah.

It is interesting to examine the laws in Exodus and Deuteronomy to see how many directives there are concerning the care of the poor, the stranger, the widow and orphan, and the person who is unable to defend himself (e.g. Exodus 22:21ff.; Deuteronomy 27:19). It was the obligation of the covenant brother to reach out to the person in need, take up the cudgel and defend him from whatever enemy tormented him — sickness, hunger, loneliness, injustice, or physical persecution.

Thus the time of Jeroboam II and the prophet Hosea can best be characterized as an era of lavish degeneracy and opulent wickedness, gluttonous materialism and family disintegration. After Jeroboam, what we see in the prophecy of Hosea are the last few swirls as the kingdom of Israel goes down the drain.

The Rise of Assyrian Power

There were only thirty years between the death of Jeroboam and the utter collapse of the kingdom of Israel before the Assyrian power. For about a hundred years the Assyrians had not been dominant along the Mediterranean coast. The strength of an ancient power was measured by her ability to conquer, and when Assyria was not making expeditions toward the coast it was likely that she was having trouble close to home. She was hedged by hostile people on the east in the mountains of the territory that we know as Iran, and she was bounded by unfriendly people on the north in the land of Urartu, modern Armenia. To the im-

mediate west was only desert, and there was nothing to conquer there. The Persian Gulf lay to the south but was no
prize for the Assyrians because they were not a maritime
nation. Fenced by mountains on the east and north, by desert
on the west, and by the gulf on the south, her only gateway
to expansion was to the northwest, along the Euphrates.

The Assyrians timed their marches annually. When they
were not having problems with their neighbors at home,
they moved out each year in systematic march. Located on
the Tigris with their capital at Nineveh, they would move
north, up the Euphrates into Syria, and then would sweep
down to the Jordan valley or down the coastal plain in
order to harass the land of Palestine.

The problems of logistics were serious in an ancient
army — there were no K-rations. Lines of supply stretched
five or six hundred miles from Assyria to the coast of the
Mediterranean. It was necessary to wait until after the spring
rains when the roads were passable and the weather dry
enough to move chariots and troops. The best plan was to
get to Palestine before the summer crops were harvested
and do the enemy the great favor of harvesting his crops for
him. And so, between the spring rains and the harvesting
of the summer crops, the Assyrians would be on the march
each year. For almost two hundred years of their history
their records chronicled the campaigns they engaged in every
spring.

Jeroboam's kingdom could flourish because, for nearly a
century, Assyria had been too involved in local skirmishes
to put pressure on Syria and Palestine. The close of the
reign of Jeroboam coincided with a major change in Assyrian
policy, which caused her to redirect her interests from med-

dling in the political affairs of Babylonia to westward expansion. Apparently she was able to free herself from nagging border conflicts with Urartu on the north and use her military forces for more profitable kinds of aggression in the coastal regions.

Throughout the prophecy of Hosea the Assyrians are on the horizon, posing both threat and temptation as the Israelites vacillate between resistance and capitulation. The Israelites were faced with a grave political problem. Their country was a land bridge between the Nile valley and Mesopotamia. The question was, in the politics of Israel, with whom were they to cast their lot? Within the court there were doubtless a pro-Egyptian party and a pro-Assyrian party, with representatives of each side trying to convince the king that the future of Israel lay with the country supported by their party. But Hosea was saying, "You better look up. Your future lies above."

Here was the prophet, speaking in this time of tremendous turmoil, watching the twilight of Israel's finest day. There was uncertainty as to what was going to happen after a half century of stalwart reign. Hosea envisioned Assyria as a giant that had been sleeping, whom God was stabbing awake. She was stretching herself and beginning to rise once again as a major power of the orient. It was only a few years after Jeroboam's death that Assyria renewed her westward thrusts to the coasts of Syria and Palestine. This meant trouble for the people of Israel.

The Assyrians, notorious during this period for their cruel, inhuman practices, were under the leadership of King Tiglath-pileser III, who came to power in 745 BC. The Baby-

lonians called him Pulu, and sometimes in the Bible we
see him referred to as King Pul (II Kings 15:19).

Tiglath-pileser was faced with a major problem that was
common to all conquering nations of that day: how to control a conquered people. It was one thing to engage in guer-
illa warfare, to swoop down upon an enemy citadel or camp
and carry off all the portable goods and a few of the choice
men and women for slaves. It was quite another thing to
be able to control, over long periods of time, a vanquished
people.

This barbaric king developed a process of homogenizing
the colonies by taking away the cream of one country, settling
them in another country, and replacing them with people
who were brought in from still another captive country. The
purpose of this population exchange was to thin out the
hot blood of patriotism so that national movements, revolu-
tions, and coups would be harder to come by. The religions
of the people necessarily became mixed so that there was
no national god around whom they could rally. The nobility
were often carried away, causing a leadership vacuum among
the people. This was but one page in Tiglath-pileser's book
of cruel practices.

Assyria could be thought of as an ancient counterpart
of Nazi Germany. Their ruthlessness, their inhumanity, their
power tactics, their disregard of the rights of the individual,
their casualness and carelessness in the light of human suffering, are prototypes of the Gestapo tactics.

In the midst of these circumstances, the Word of God
came to the prophet Hosea. At the very moment when it
looked as though God was absent, when Israel's future
internally was in jeopardy and her external security threat-

ened — at this very moment of crisis, God made his Word known. In spite of the degeneracy of Jeroboam's reign and the hostility of the Assyrians, in spite of the corruption of Israel's values and this resurgence of foreign power, God was sovereign.

This is the way the hand of God works. In what may seem to be an impossible situation, the sovereignty of God is performing the task of judgment and grace upon our lives, which it is his role and his privilege to perform. It is within this kind of context that Hosea speaks and reminds us that there is no hour so dark that God's hand cannot be seen in it. God is not bound by our circumstances; he is sovereign over them. He used the Assyrians for his own purposes and triumphed in the midst of Israelite corruption.

As we look at the continual striving among nations and observe what seems to be a certain decadence within ourselves as a people, a certain purposeless striving, a certain frenetic searching to discover who we are so that we will know what we ought to be against these external threats, let us remember Hosea's message and Hosea's God. God is neither deaf nor lacking in strength and, as has happened so many times in history, as we look to God, what appears to be our darkest hour may prove to be our finest.

Chapter Three

THE TIMES THAT SHAPED THE MESSAGE:
COLLAPSE FROM WITHIN

> They made kings, but not through me.
>> They set up princes, but without my knowledge.
> With their silver and gold they made idols
>> for their own destruction.
>
> (Hosea 8:4)

The Assyrian threat from without was matched by Israel's inner collapse. This was a time of strategy and counter-strategy, of intrigue and counter-intrigue; and this seething, smoldering atmosphere is likened by the poet-prophet Hosea to an oven which is being prepared to receive the dough and to bake the bread:

> For like an oven their hearts burn with intrigue;
>> all night their anger smolders;
>> in the morning it blazes like a flaming fire.
> All of them are hot as an oven,
>> and they devour their rulers.
> All their kings have fallen;
>> and none of them calls upon me.
>
> (7:6-7)

This is Hosea's summary of the state of affairs in the kingdom of Israel during the time of his prophetic ministry. This tragic story is related in II Kings:

In the thirty-eighth year of Azariah king of Judah Zechariah

> the son of Jeroboam reigned over Israel in Samaria six months.
> And he did what was evil in the sight of the Lord, as his
> fathers had done. He did not depart from the sins of Jeroboam
> the son of Nebat, which he made Israel to sin. Shallum the
> son of Jabesh conspired against him, and struck him down
> at Ibleam, and killed him, and reigned in his stead.
>
> (II Kings 15:8-10)

Then followed a treacherous game of royal musical chairs
in which five kings were overthrown and succeeded within
a twelve-year period. (See chart, p. 111). This is exactly what
Hosea is describing when he says,

> and they devour their rulers.
> All their kings have fallen;
> and none of them calls upon me.
>
> (7:7)

This internal political scene was one of confusion brought
about by several factors: the instability of the northern kingdom, the power politics of the eighth century, and Israel's
social, moral, and spiritual corruption.

Instability of the Northern Kingdom

The northern kingdom of Israel and the southern kingdom of Judah stand in bold contrast to each other in dynastic continuity. From the time that Solomon ascended
the throne about 970 bc to the time that Zedekiah was taken
into captivity in 586, there was a son of David on the throne
of Judah in fulfillment of the prophecy which Nathan had
given at the outset of his royal ministry (II Samuel 7:4-16).
This does not mean that all was well within the southern
kingdom, but it does mean that there was a kind of political
stability which the northern kingdom never knew.

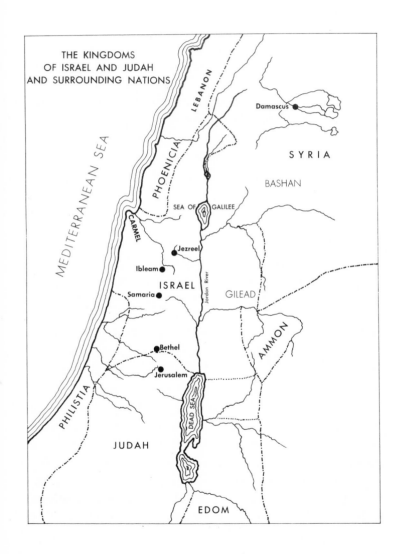

THE KINGDOMS
OF ISRAEL AND JUDAH
AND SURROUNDING NATIONS

LEBANON

Damascus

SYRIA

PHOENICIA

BASHAN

MEDITERRANEAN SEA

CARMEL

SEA OF GALILEE

Jezreel

Ibleam

ISRAEL

Jordan River

GILEAD

Samaria

Bethel

AMMON

Jerusalem

PHILISTIA

DEAD SEA

JUDAH

EDOM

The northern kingdom was born in revolution at the time of Jeroboam I, who led an insurrection against the absurd and tyrannical policies of Rehoboam, the son of Solomon. But Jeroboam's family was unable to retain its hold on the throne, and a pattern of dynastic unsettledness marked the northern kingdom for most of its violent and turbulent history. Jehu's dynasty, of which Jeroboam II was the fourth ruler, was itself born in blood (II Kings 9:1–10:31).

So there was always the danger of revolution, always the threat of assassination. The stresses and strains that were inbuilt in the northern kingdom came to the surface under the menacing advances of Assyria and the collapse of Jeroboam's dynasty.

Power Politics of the Times

The land bridge that connected the Nile valley and the Mesopotamian valley was considered a strategic territory. Its importance lay in the fact that whichever country could control the land bridge could dominate the other valley. Consequently, there had been a never ending struggle for control of this area (in which Palestine was located) for at least a millennium before the time of Hosea. And even today this territory is no stranger to intrigue.

Within the northern kingdom there were strong political influences fighting to be in the driver's seat, trying to take over the reins of a runaway government, and pointing it toward Assyria or toward Egypt. This often resulted in coups that placed either a pro-Assyrian or a pro-Egyptian king on the throne of Israel. Hosea's concern over this political confusion is expressed in passages like 5:13 and 7:11.

Moral and Spiritual Corruption of Israel

A third factor that added to the generally chaotic conditions was the social, moral, and spiritual corruption of the people. They were inherently weak because they had flouted the laws of God and considered the Ten Commandments dispensable when expediency demanded their suspension.

It is axiomatic — and Hosea would stress this — that man breaks the law of God only in turn to be broken by that law. This cavalier attitude toward the commandments contributed to the collapse of the northern kingdom. When the principles of justice of ancient Israel, the rights of the individual, and the values of honesty, uprightness, and fair play were disregarded, it was only a question of which king would be the victim of the next intrigue and from which source this intrigue would come. A nation cannot defy the laws of God and not have such defiance affect the political stability of the land. What we do morally and spiritually will ultimately take its toll on what we are politically.

Perhaps the most significant factor in the collapse of Israel was the moral and spiritual degeneracy of the people. The best summary of these problems is to be found in the fourth chapter. In this passage Hosea is actually borrowing legal terminology. His oracle is framed in the language of the law court:

> Hear the word of the Lord (Order in the court!), O people of Israel; for the Lord has a controversy (he is making his case) with the inhabitants of the land. (Now here is the case:) There is no faithfulness (he cannot depend on their word) or kindness (the old covenant ideal which reached out to the neighbor who was in need, which protected the rights of the poor and the widow and the orphan, was being violated), and no

knowledge of God in the land (the relationship of obedience, of trust, of love, which the prophet describes as the knowledge of God, was absent).

(4:1)

Instead, this is what was found, and the echo of the Ten Commandments can be heard behind this indictment:

There is swearing ("You shall not take the name of the Lord your God in vain"), lying ("You shall not bear false witness . . ."), killing ("You shall not kill"), stealing ("You shall not steal"), committing adultery ("You shall not commit adultery"); they break all bounds and murder follows murder.

(4:2)

This was the religious and social situation in the land of Israel as summarized by Hosea.

This period of Hosea's ministry, from about 740 to 725 BC, was probably the most idolatrous period in all of Israel's history. Hosea speaks out against this idolatry in the strongest terms. He brands it *spiritual harlotry,* and the entire first three chapters are dedicated to this theme. The tone for the book is set in 1:2:

When the Lord first spoke through Hosea, the Lord said to Hosea, "Go, take a wife of harlotry and have children of harlotry, for the land commits great harlotry by forsaking the Lord."

Hosea's message tells us that the relationship between God and his people can be likened to a marriage relationship. There was a marriage ceremony at the foot of Sinai, where the people of Israel pledged themselves to have and to hold from that day forward, for richer, for poorer, for better, for worse, in sickness and in health, forsaking all others, cleaving only to God so long as they would live.

When the question was put to the children of Israel,

they said, "I do." But as soon as they moved into the land, they began to corrupt themselves with idols. When they were seduced into the false religious practices of the Canaanites, they were actually committing spiritual adultery. They came to believe that the Canaanite fertility god, Baal, was responsible for the productivity of their land, for the very food they ate. Because they believed that they were gaining material benefits from this Baal-worship, it became a kind of spiritual prostitution, practiced through lust and for material gain.

This is the kind of idolatry of which Hosea speaks, an idolatry which had its beginning in the time of Jeroboam I. In the days of David and Solomon, before the division of the kingdom, Jerusalem was the capital of the land and its temple was the center of worship. After the kingdom split, it was politically infeasible to have the Israelites going down to another kingdom to worship. Jeroboam solved this problem by building rival shrines at Dan in the north and Bethel in the south.

In these shrines there were golden calves which were not at first intended to be idols. They were considered pedestals on which the invisible deity, the Lord of Israel, would enthrone himself. But because the Canaanites worshiped idols, and because one of the characteristic forms of idolatry was a calf (the symbol of the vigor and vitality of the fertility god), what had started out to be a pedestal for the invisible Lord became a substitute for him.

The prophets brought several serious charges against this kind of idolatry. They felt that the people should have been worshiping God at the Jerusalem temple (proposed by David and built by Solomon), which had been the national center of worship before the division of the kingdom.

Another reason that the prophets spoke out against idolatry was that idolatry, by definition, involves caricature. In Isaiah forty, the prophet points out the futility of likening any creature or thing to an incomparable God. Make any likeness of God, Isaiah says, and to a certain extent it is going to be a caricature because God defies representation. Whether we try to draw his picture, or identify him with the sun or the storm clouds, or make some image to represent his being, we are deceiving ourselves — and blaspheming him — because we are representing him in terms that are unworthy of his person.

They also spoke out against idolatry because there were many customs related to these idolatrous practices which stabbed at the heart of the true faith of Israel. For instance, the people who engaged in idolatry were using it as a means of reading the mind of God:

> My people inquire of a thing of wood,
>   and their staff gives them oracles.
> For a spirit of harlotry has led them astray,
>   and they have left their God to play the harlot.
>   (4:12)

This was an ironic situation: here were the covenant people into whose midst God had sent his watchmen and messengers, the prophets; here were the covenant people to whom God had promised to reveal his will. The prophetic office was part of God's pledge to the spiritual welfare of the Israelites. Moses announced that God would "raise up ...a prophet like me" (Deuteronomy 18:15). But when the prophets attempted to point the people to God, and to reveal his will to them, they were ignored or rejected. Instead, the Israelites turned to such things as ouija boards and divining rods.

To the sorrow of the prophets, many other pagan practices had penetrated society. Drunkenness was a problem: "Wine and new wine take away the understanding" (4:11). Baal was considered lord of the vine. It was he who made the grapes come forth every year in all of their succulent abundance. What better way to celebrate and give thanks for this great gift of the god Baal than by enjoying it to the full and indulging in drunkenness.

Masochism played a part in their rites and rituals. When the people had some special request to make, and particularly when they wanted God to send a good harvest, they held ceremonies of wailing and weeping something like professional mourners. The prophet says:

> They do not cry to me from the heart,
>   but they wail upon their beds;
> for grain and wine they gash themselves,
>   they rebel against me.
>
> (7:14)

This brings to mind the scene on Mt. Carmel, that dramatic watershed in the history of Israel where Elijah, lone and sturdy, put his proposition to the 450 prophets of Baal: "The God who answers by fire, he is God" (I Kings 18:24). What were the prophets of Baal doing? They were wailing, they were mourning, they were gashing themselves as if somehow, by the flow of their own blood, by their own self-torture, they could bend the arm of deity. The Israelites, who had ready access to God, who could come boldly before the throne of grace if they came with a whole heart, were engaging in these same practices.

Another immoral custom was the process of sacred prostitution. Baal was the Canaanite god of fertility. He was responsible for the blossoms of the almonds in February, and for the sending out of the barley shoots in March; he was responsible for the ewes casting their lambs and the cows their calves in March and April.

Baal produced this kind of fertility in the same way that fertility was produced on the human or animal level — by sexual intercourse. There was a goddess, Anat, who was considered to be Baal's consort, and it was believed that when he copulated with her, fertility would result in the land. In order to be sure that Baal would engage in this cosmic act of intercourse, these degenerate Israelites and Canaanites practiced a kind of imitative magic. When they wanted rain, they poured out water on the ground as a rain-making ceremony; when they wanted to afflict or destroy someone who was their enemy, they made an image of his person and then broke the image. So if they wanted to assure green growth, abundant fruit, and well-stocked herds, they practiced religious prostitution.

This is why Hosea so often uses the figure of harlotry. He says:

> They sacrifice on the tops of the mountains,
>   and make offerings upon the hills,
> under oak, poplar, and terebinth,
>   because their shade is good.
> Therefore your daughters play the harlot,
>   and your brides commit adultery.
> I will not punish your daughters when they play
>   the harlot,
>   nor your brides when they commit adultery;
> for the men themselves go aside with harlots,

and sacrifice with cult prostitutes,
and a people without understanding shall come
to ruin.

(4:13, 14)

This was the tragic situation described in the book of Hosea: religious apostasy, political confusion, and social corruption. Yet even in the midst of this darkness, God's sovereign hand was seen.

If God could work in the times of Hosea, perhaps this can remind us that no circumstances need be beyond his redeeming. He does not need an optimum situation in which to carry on his program. He can bring hope into the hopeless experiences of life. Furthermore, hours that seem dark with his judgment may lead to times that are bright with his grace. His judgment may be designed to lead us to seek his forgiveness. As Hosea puts it:

Come, let us return to the Lord;
for he has torn, that he may heal us;
he has stricken, and he will bind us up.

(6:1)

The problem of idolatry is not one that can be limited to the times and circumstances of Hosea or Isaiah or Jeremiah. It is a very characteristically human problem in the wide spectrum of human problems. Our tendency toward idolatry as people is so subtle and so ingrained, it is so much a part of our human predicament and our human rebellion, that it may be at the very time that we feel we have reached the summit of spiritual success that we find ourselves plunging over the brink into the abyss of idolatrous pride. All that idolatry involves is making something other than God absolute. It is giving ultimate allegiance to a person or thing or idea that is not ultimate.

It is always easier for us to see the idolatrous tendencies of others than to see our own. We are apt to feel that our particular cause is the kingdom of God. We fail to bring it under the censure of the Word and the Spirit, assuming that because we are "orthodox" we must be right. When we do this we are idolaters.

As in the days of Hosea, so now a continuing experience of worship and repentance is absolutely necessary to act as an anti-idolatrous influence in our lives. If we fail to worship God, if we fail to confess our sins and to repent; if we fail to acknowledge our own unworthiness, our emptiness apart from the vitality of God, we are idol-worshipers because something other than God is on the pedestal of our lives.

Our idols may not take the gross forms that existed in the days of Hosea. Our golden calves may be a subtle kind of self-righteousness — or a reliance on our own abilities that leaves God out of the picture. It may be a theologian's belief that he is the best interpreter of God's truth. It may be our conviction that we know the best way to witness as a Christian, or our feeling that we belong to the best kind of Christian organization. Any time we give first priority to that which should not come first, any time we treat our finite ideas with infinite seriousness, we are guilty of idolatry.

We are all worshipers of one kind or another. There is no man alive who does not have in his life "sacred" areas that one dare not laugh at, jest about or chide him for, areas that one dare not pinch or poke because they are too tender. With one it may be concern for material goods or obsession to advance in business; with another, membership in a club or organization or pride of ancestry. Such persons are intensely religious whether they profess to be or not. It is part of our nature to be religious. We put something at the center of our lives and pivot around it.

What the prophets are saying is, "You are going to have an ultimate concern; make sure it is concern about the Ultimate. You are going to give final authority to someone in your life; make sure it is the One who is worthy of final authority."

Hosea brings to us a warning against idolatry, not only in the pagan islands of the sea where men bow down to wood and stone but in the hearts and minds of men everywhere who confuse their own notions with the will and Word of God and fail to open their hearts to his grace, which is the sustenance of Christian life.

Chapter Four

THE MARRIAGE AND THE MESSAGE

I will heal their faithlessness;
I will love them freely.
(Hosea 14:4)

Few Old Testament passages have been more thought-provoking than the beginning chapters of Hosea. The demand of God upon Hosea is unique:

"Go, take to yourself a wife of harlotry and have children of harlotry, for the land commits great harlotry by forsaking the Lord."

(1:2)

The details are few, and the whole episode is recounted in such condensed fashion that a great deal is left to the imagination. But neither the details nor the story's meaning is merely academic; they are the foundation of Hosea's ministry.

A prophet was called to bear a cross, to demonstrate in his own experience both the suffering heart and the redeeming love of God. With unflinching obedience Hosea drank a bitter cup. In bending to a will not his own he left the most poignant Old Testament illustration of divine love, which helped to prepare the way for the coming of the One who in fullest measure embodied this love.

Hosea's Call

Desperate situations sometimes call for drastic measures. The combination of corruption and luxury throughout Jeroboam's lengthy reign had brought Israel to a state of spiritual and moral bankruptcy. Baal-worship, which had been introduced officially by Ahab's queen, Jezebel, was still rampant in the land despite Jehu's effort to wipe it out. In turning to the Baals, Israel had played false with her First Love. It was in order to illustrate memorably this spiritual adultery that God commanded Hosea to marry a "wife of harlotry," a woman of ill repute.

Some scholars theorize that the relationship of Hosea and Gomer must have been pure at first, just as Israel's relationship with God was pure in the Exodus experiences:

> I remember the devotion of your youth,
> your love as a bride,
> how you followed me in the wilderness,
> in a land not sown.
> Israel was holy to the Lord,
> the first fruits of his harvest.
> (Jeremiah 2:2-3)

It should be pointed out, however, that Hosea's marriage with Gomer was not meant to recapitulate God's dealings with Israel but to thrust into sharp relief Israel's present degeneracy. Its purpose was to highlight the bleakness of the times, to testify against the degradation of the hour in which he was living. How could this be done more effectively and dramatically than by a marriage between a prophet and a wicked woman? The text says:

> So he went and took Gomer the daughter of Diblaim, and she conceived and bore him a son.
> (1:3)

Quite clearly Hosea associated his prophetic call with his marriage to Gomer; however, the question of which came first is puzzling. Was he called to be a prophet before the marriage, or did his call grow out of his experience with Gomer?

If we take the words of 1:2 at face value, and it seems best to do so, his call came immediately before he married. His prophetic act in naming the first son Jezreel is strong evidence for the view that he was already a prophet at the time of his marriage. There can be no doubt, however, that his tragic experiences with Gomer had a profound influence upon him, refining his character and enriching his ministry. In a sense, then, his call was a continuous one, beginning before he took Gomer and growing and deepening throughout the years of his suffering.

Hosea's Wife

What kind of woman was Gomer? What was the meaning of God's command, "Go, take to yourself a wife of harlotry"? The theories offered by Biblical scholars are many and varied. Some believe this harlotry consisted of Baal-worship or religious fornication. Gomer, on the basis of this interpretation, would be called a wife of harlotry not because she was an immoral woman, but because she belonged to an idolatrous or spiritually adulterous people. This desire to protect Gomer's reputation stems, in part, from the moral problem involved in God's command and Hosea's response to it.

To ease this problem, some have held that Gomer was not wicked when Hosea married her but turned to evil afterwards. The command in 1:2, then, would represent not the actual wording of God's call but Hosea's interpretation of it in retrospect. Those who hold this view theorize that in looking back over the years Hosea realized that the call of God came to him when he took his wife, a wife who proved as unfaithful to him as Israel had to God. They contend that if Gomer was evil at the time of her marriage, her husband knew nothing about this. Even if this approach were acceptable for chapter one, chapter three would present a problem: here Hosea knows full well what kind of woman he is taking.

In recent years it has become popular to consider Gomer a cult prostitute, a devotee of the fertility rites of Baal. Although this is a possibility, it is by no means certain. She is called an adulteress in 3:1, and the technical Hebrew term for religious harlot is nowhere used of her. Further, it is not likely that marriage to such a person would have been any less distasteful to Hosea, who scathingly denounces cult prostitution, than marriage to an ordinary harlot.

The interpretation that seems most reasonable is that Gomer was a notoriously wicked woman whom God chose for marriage to Hosea as a drastic and dramatic means of putting a message across. This interpretation permits a more literal, face-value acceptance of the story.

The commands of God in Scripture frequently prove grievous. Isaiah at one point in his life was asked to walk around the streets of Jerusalem for three years wearing nothing but a loin cloth, an offense to oriental standards of modesty, and a laughing-stock to the people (Isaiah 20:2ff.). Jeremiah was asked by God to remain single, to refrain from marrying, as a symbol of the disrupted life which the people of Judah were going to live in captivity and exile (Jeremiah

16:1ff.). This was a burdensome cross to add to the ones that Jeremiah was already carrying. The Old Testament, and oriental society as a whole, placed strong emphasis upon both marriage and childbearing: "Happy is the man who has his quiver full of them" (Psalm 127:5). The perpetuation of the family name was important. Furthermore, laws against homosexuality were stringent, and a man who refused to marry was open to suspicion of being a homosexual. This gives us some idea of the degree of personal sacrifice that was involved in Jeremiah's act of obedience to God's command.

And so Hosea's experience in receiving this kind of command was not unique within Scripture. These were times when God required the prophets to do extraordinary things and make unusual sacrifices in order to etch indelibly his message of grace or judgment upon the hearts of the people.

Hosea's Children

The three children symbolize God's judgment upon Israel. Notice their names. The first son was called Jezreel (1:4). The explanation given is that the house of Jehu, the ruling house of Israel, will be punished for the blood of Jezreel. This is a grim reference to an incident in the history of Israel. It was at the instigation of the prophet Elisha that a young, hard-driving general named Jehu, commander-in-chief of the army of Israel, was ordered to lead a coup against King Joram. Jehu carried out his assignment with a vengeance. It was not enough for him to murder the king; he wiped out the entire royal family and conducted a wholesale slaughter against the priests and worshipers of

Baal. Because Jehu's motives had turned sour, and he could not maintain his position of power in humility and selflessness, judgment had to take place. And so God told Hosea that the house of Jehu was going to be avenged for the blood of Jezreel. In fulfillment of this prophecy, Jeroboam's son, Zechariah, was killed in this valley of Jezreel.

The second child, a daughter, was called Lo-ruhamah, "not pitied." She symbolized the fact that God was going to turn his back for a time on the house of Israel and withhold his pity from them.

The third child was called Lo-ammi, "not my people"; and he represented the gulf between God and Israel, a chasm not of God's making but of Israel's. Israel had defected from a relationship with God; he had refused to act as His people, and God was going to force Israel to collect the wages of his own sinful choice.

Hosea's People

After the three children were born, it appears that Gomer turned to other lovers:

> Say to your brother, "My people," and to your
>   sister, "She has obtained pity."
> Plead with your mother, plead —
>   for she is not my wife,
>   and I am not her husband —
> that she put away her harlotry from her face,
>   and her adultery from between her breasts;
> lest I strip her naked
>   and make her as in the day she was born. . . .
>   (2:1-3)

This was a customary way of treating a woman who was being divorced because of immorality. To be stripped naked would be the worst kind of shame into which she could fall in a Middle Eastern culture.

As the chapter proceeds, Gomer fades out of the picture and the Israelites' infidelity receives the spotlight as they lavish their worship on the Baals (who are the "lovers" mentioned in 2:5) without realizing that it was not Baal but God who had blessed them abundantly:

> And she did not know
>> that it was I who gave her
>> the grain, the wine, and the oil,
> and who lavished upon her silver
>> and gold which they used for Baal.
>>> (2:8)

An assessment of the crimes of Israel against God is given (2:9-13) and sentence is pronounced in strong terms:

> I will take back *my* grain.... I will take away *my* wool....
> I will lay waste her vines.... I will punish her for the feast
> days of the Baals....

This is an indictment of their misdirected worship and thanksgiving and a prediction of devastation, which would come in the form of famine due to drought and locusts.

It is interesting to note that the punishment is directly related to the crime. The crops which Israel credited to Baal, the fertility god, were marked for devastation:

> And I will lay waste her vines and her fig trees,
>> of which she said,
> "These are my hire,
>> which my lovers have given me."
> I will make them a forest,
>> and the beasts of the field shall devour them.
>>> (2:12)

The complete capitulation of Israel to the Assyrians became the judgment predicted in this passage.

God's Initiative

A major turning point occurs in verse 14. "Therefore," which usually heralds judgment in the writings of the prophets, announces, instead, a message of mercy. God in his steadfast love has taken the initiative in forgiveness and, in due time, grace will follow judgment. A new covenant is foretold, with all nature joining in the scene of reconciliation. The promise of verse 20, "I will betroth you to me in faithfulness; and you shall know the Lord," is an indication that a new marriage relationship will take place between God and Israel by the restoring grace of God.

Hosea's Response

Then God commanded Hosea to follow His example of forgiveness and return Gomer to her place as his wife (3:1). He was told, significantly, not only to take her back but to love her.

One can well imagine the conflicts that must have raged within Hosea. Even to befriend a harlot, let alone marry her, meant public shame for one whose calling compelled him to walk in integrity. And what a blow to the pride of any man to have a wife scorn his love and wantonly pursue other lovers. How tempted he must have been to wash his hands of the sordid mess and console himself with the thought that he had done his best, and surely God would understand his refusal to remarry this woman.

But at this point we see a sharp difference between the

way of man committed to fulfilling his own desires and the way of man committed to obeying the will of God.

Yet even the reconciliation involved discipline (3:3-5). The sin had been serious — both Gomer's and Israel's — and a period of probation was necessary in both cases before a complete relationship could be enjoyed. In their time of exile, the Israelites had to learn to do without the royal leadership which had so often led them astray and the formal worship which had degenerated into idolatry. In this way God sought to bring home to a prodigal people the severity of their sin and to draw them to the point of desiring and seeking a reunion with him. As for Gomer, she had to refrain from all sexual relations even with her husband, an appropriate punishment for a woman who had been so consumed with the sensual.

The order of events is important: after indicting Israel and passing sentence on her, God pledges his forgiveness, and Hosea learns from him to forgive; God takes the lead in restoration, and Hosea follows suit.

The theology of the story would be ruined if Hosea had taken Gomer back first, as if God somehow learned forgiveness by seeing what Hosea did. But the story makes it clear that, when it comes to forgiveness, it is God who sets the pace. His word to Hosea and to people of all times is, "Go thou and do likewise." The Apostle Paul brings the same injunction: "Be kind to one another, tenderhearted, forgiving one another, as God in Christ forgave you" (Ephesians 4:32).

How do we learn forgiveness? By being forgiven. How

do we learn to accept the person who has sinned against us? By remembering that we ourselves have been accepted. How do we learn to live graciously? By taking seriously in our own lives the meaning of grace. A harsh, hypercritical person who cannot accept the faults and mistakes of others is most likely a person who at the depths of his personality has never really *experienced* forgiveness. He has never really been able to accept himself as forgiven and, having been unable to accept himself as forgiven, has never learned how to reach out to others in true forgiveness. God is the pioneer of forgiveness; it is he who blazes the trail. He says to Hosea, and to us, "Now *you* demonstrate to all people what kind of God I am by doing the same thing in your own experience."

When I have sinned against someone —

Do I recognize that I have sinned against God as well as man and seek the pardon of both?

Do I completely acknowledge my guilt or do I hedge my repentance with excuses?

Am I truly contrite?

Do I make every effort to repair whatever damage my thoughtlessness or cruelty may have caused?

When I have been sinned against —

Am I willing to take the initiative in restoration of fellowship?

Am I anxious to forget the offense or is it "forgiven but not forgotten"?

Do I forgive in humble spirit, without condescension, or do I exact my pound of flesh?

Forgiveness is the only road to restored fellowship. It clears the air of guilt and despair and brings fresh meaning to life. Neither pride nor frustration can be present when forgiveness takes over. It is God's way of coping with our waywardness and showing us the only way to establish a mature relationship with him and with each other.

There is a sense in which Hosea gives us a *preview of the cross.* He was a cross-bearer, a man who was wounded for the transgressions of others, who was bruised for their iniquities. The redemptive suffering of Christ becomes more meaningful to us as we vicariously share the experience of Hosea, whose home became his Gethsemane, whose marriage became his Calvary. Many times he must have wished this cup taken from him. Yet the great "nevertheless"— *Thy will be done* — became his rule of life, as it must become ours.

We see from the book of Hosea that suffering is not necessarily deserved. There is never any hint that it was Hosea's fault that Gomer went astray, that he was responsible. Here you have a picture of innocent suffering, suffering beyond that which the circumstances seem to warrant.

And so we perceive from Hosea's experience that suffering, in God's broad view, may well have a higher purpose than punishment. It may teach us lessons that can be learned no other way; it may give tone to our character that would otherwise stay limp and flabby; it may make our lives vibrant testimonies to God's steadfastness in an unsteady age. The person who can live trustingly and graciously in the midst of suffering can have a special ministry in a world that so often is embittered or broken by it.

Now in this example of suffering, God is preparing the way for our understanding of the cross of Jesus Christ. On the cross Christ, the most righteous man in history, became history's greatest sufferer. At the cross God worked out redemption through innocent suffering. For it cannot be said that Christ suffered because he sinned. This is the way that God chose to exact the penalty for our sins, to deal fully and finally with them, and to write his love clearly and firmly before us.

If we try to understand the cross of Christ without first seeing it against the kind of background that Hosea gives, it presents us with a kind of thorny problem: "Why did it have to happen? Surely this is a righteous man. This fellow didn't deserve this." The world looks at the cross this way because it does not know the God of Hosea, the God of the prophets, the God who works his will in history in ways that are beyond our ken. Loving redemption, redemption at the tremendous cost of a person's reputation, even of his own life, was already anticipated in the experience of the prophet Hosea.

In portraying the marriage between God and Israel, Hosea builds upon the foundation of the creation story, which gives us some hints about *purposes in marriage* in addition to procreation:

> So God created man in his own image, in the image of God he created him; male and female he created them.
>
> (Genesis 1:27)

The last statement appears to be a comment on the first two clauses. There seems to be a definite connection between the image of God, man's relationship to God, his capacity for conversation with God (which is evident throughout the first three chapters of Genesis), and the relationship between man and woman.

The male-female relationship was designed by God from the beginning not merely to perpetuate the race but to mirror God's relationship with man. The intimate character of marriage is highlighted in the creation of Eve, who is actually fashioned out of Adam, as well as in the specific command that marriage is to take precedence over all other family relationships (Genesis 2:23-24).

Hosea uses his marriage to illustrate the union between God and Israel and, in doing so, draws light from the creation narrative. But he does something more. He anticipates and prepares for Paul's profound observations concerning the marital bond between Christ and the Church:

> For the husband is the head of the wife as Christ is the head of the church ... (Ephesians 5:23).
> As the church is subject to Christ, so let wives also be subject in everything to their husbands ... (5:24).
> Husbands, love your wives as Christ loved the church ... (5:25).

Paul grounds this analogy in Genesis 2:24, which stresses the exclusive nature of the marriage union. Hosea sounds this same note of exclusiveness when he labels Israel's idolatry as harlotry and contrasts it with God's relentless loyalty to his people. In a sense Hosea is a bridge between Genesis and the New Testament. He takes an idea implicit in the creation story and applies it explicitly to the marriage between God and Israel. Then Paul gives the relationship a distinctively Christian turn as he applies it to Christ's union with the new Israel, the new people of God, the Church.

Marriage takes on fresh significance in the light of these passages. The relationship of husband and wife becomes a reflection of God's love for his people and their devotion to him. Loyal, steadfast love helps to overcome the tensions that threaten to separate two people. They are pledged to each other after the pattern of God's covenant with his people, and from him they learn to work out the meaning of this pledge.

There are times when marital stress and strain set in, when family problems seem insurmountable, when one is tempted to lay aside a particular cross and escape into a life of irresponsibility and self-seeking. Hosea dramatically demonstrates that the godly life involves sacrificial living:

> . . . he who does not take his cross and follow me is not worthy of me. He who finds his life will lose it, and he who loses his life for my sake will find it (Matthew 10:38-39).

People learn more from what we do than from what we say. Emerson said, "What you are stands over you the while, and thunders so that I cannot hear what you say to the contrary." Hosea could have preached the love of God from every pulpit in the land and his message would not have had the impact that it had when he himself worked out within the four walls of his own home the meaning of redemptive love.

Every day of our lives we are dealing with people, including our families, who need to see in us demonstrations of a steadfast, God-like love — a love which does not require response in kind, which does not, as Shakespeare put it, "alter when it alteration finds." We can theorize and philosophize at great length about the importance of Christian love, but if our theories do not become facts, and our philosophy does not in reality become our way of life, our Christianity is cold and empty.

People have a feeling for the genuineness of our love

that is more sensitive than radar. For us to be able to love the unlovely — the churlish boss, the carping wife, the peevish child, the irate neighbor — means that we have learned something of what God's love is all about.

Chapter Five

THE HOLY ONE OF ISRAEL

For I am God and not man,
the Holy One in your midst.
(Hosea 11:9)

Hosea, more than most prophets, illuminates the inner recesses of God's personality. He shows us God, the Father, agonizing over Israel, the wayward child. We see something of the concern, something of the conflict within the heart of God. Hosea's relationship with Gomer was an analogy of God's relationship with Israel. As he was sinned against by his wife, so God had been sinned against. As God reached out to forgive and restore Israel, so Hosea forgave Gomer.

God used the tribulations of Hosea to give a better picture of his own nature. The tragic events of Hosea's life lend emphasis to the fact that God works out his revelation through human experience and through human personality. Wherever one turns the pages of history, there God is speaking through people; there God is working in the lives of men. But this is perceived only by the eye of faith; it is not open to logical demonstration or scientific investigation.

The Bible stands in direct contrast to other religious documents, and the Biblical faith differs markedly from other religious approaches. When we open the Bible, for instance,

we find that God is there. He is not defined, because to define is, literally, to limit; God in his infinity cannot be defined by finite man.

If one were to attempt to define God, one would start,
God is — but then what do you say after that? You could try,
God is a person — but he cannot be linked too closely to
personality as we know personality, with all of its limitations
and imperfections. God is a being — but this is merely another way of stating the fact that he exists. God is a spirit —
but to stop at this point is to suggest that he is but one among
many other spirits. The uniqueness of God always poses problems when we try to define who he is.

The Bible makes descriptive statements about God: God
is love, God is truth, God is a consuming fire. But these are
not definitions. They deal with some aspect of God's nature,
but there is no category to which God may be consigned.
God's uniqueness sets him apart from every being, from every
other person, from every other object or subject within the
universe.

So when the Bible talks about God, it defines God by
demonstration. What is God? He is the One who in the be-
ginning created the heavens and the earth. What is God?
He is the One who led Abraham out of Ur of the Chaldeans.
What is God? He is the One who became flesh in Jesus
Christ.

The Bible confronts us with God and in doing so stands
in direct contrast to all attempts to analyze the nature of
reality that are found in other religions. The Bible defies
all efforts to speculate on the nature of God. The Bible puts
the lie to those religions which see God as the object of man's
discovery. The Eureka! that the Bible shouts is not so much

that man has found God, but that God has found man. The discovery is God's breaking in on us, not our reaching up to him.

Even when the Bible urges men to seek the Lord, it does not mean that they are to start from scratch, but rather that they are to respond to One who has already made himself known to them in Israel's history and in Jesus Christ.

God Takes the Initiative

The Bible stresses the *divine initiative* from the beginning. It is God who speaks, and creation takes place. It is God who makes man and puts him in a garden. It is God who searches for man after man has sinned against him. It is God who says to Noah, "I am going to send a flood. You build an ark." It is God who says to Moses, "I want you to go down to Egypt," and to the Israelites, "I want you to come out of Egypt." Hosea stands firmly in this Biblical tradition.

God first spoke to Hosea and said, "Go, take to yourself a wife..." (1:2). This was not Hosea wrestling in agony with the problem of Israel's rebellion and coming to some conclusion. This was God reaching down into the experience of Hosea and guiding him along a pilgrim road according to divine plan. The prophet has no firmer conviction than the conviction, "Thus saith the Lord."

It is difficult to understand the nature of this conviction. As far as we can tell, Hosea was not a visionary who in mystic contemplation saw the anguish of his people, God's judgment, and then future restoration. He learned these things, not in an ivory tower, but in the turmoil of the kitchen with a quarrelsome wife. He learned them in the bedroom where he was confronted with his wife's unfaithfulness. It was here that God took the initiative and spoke to him.

And this is the way God speaks to us. It is not some evolutionary process through which we pass. It is not even some great discovery, some stroke of genius like Archimedes' discovery of the principle of specific gravity or the use of fulcrum and lever. It is not the product of human intelligence or human instinct. It is God meeting us in the midst of our circumstances. And it is our rebellion, our fleeing from him, our hard-heartedness, that make this kind of personal confrontation necessary. If God does not speak to us, we can know nothing about him. The Christian religion is based on God's disclosure of his nature and his will to man. God takes the initiative in this, Hosea tells us, and maintains it at every point.

God takes the initiative in creation. The Hebrews were not scientific farmers. They knew nothing about artificial fertilizer, hybridization of seed, or automated silage, but they did know that when they planted something and took care of it they reaped what they had sown. They knew the biological process that caused their cows to cast calves and their ewes to cast lambs. They knew the pattern of conception, pregnancy, and birth within the human family. While they did not minimize human agency or human ingenuity, the belief that God was involved in all creation had been instilled in them by their forefathers.

Even when the great host of Israelites had defected to the Baals, the faithful remnant kept alive the historic faith in the creating and sustaining power of God. Profound confessions of this faith are heard in the Psalms:

Thou dost cause the grass to grow for the cattle....
(Psalm 104:14)

These all look to thee,
    to give them their food in due season.
(Psalm 104:27)

Failure to recognize their complete dependence upon the true God cost the Israelites of Hosea's day dearly. They made the mistake of crediting the bounty of their crops to Baal. God says:

And she did not know
    that it was I who gave her
    the grain, the wine, and the oil,
and who lavished upon her silver
    and gold which they used for Baal.
(2:8)

God then reminds them that he who is Lord of the blessings of creation is also Lord of the blight:

And I will lay waste her vines and her fig trees,
    of which she said,
"These are my hire,
    which my lovers have given me."
I will make them a forest,
    and the beasts of the field shall devour them.
(2:12)

There is no sense in which Luther Burbank or other scientific trail blazers have made the Biblical view of God passé. Biochemistry and agronomy are technical ways of describing what happens through these natural processes, but the eye of faith sees beyond them to the divine source. It is God who is Lord of the flocks and herds; it is God who gives life to every field and orchard; all blessings flow from him.

God takes the initiative in judgment, Hosea stresses. God tells the Israelites of judgment that will come because

they have forgotten him (2:9ff.): "I will take back my grain
... I will put an end to all her mirth... I will lay waste her
vines and her fig trees... I will punish her for the feast days
of the Baals...."

As Hosea's message unfolds in chapters 4 to 14 his indictment against his people intensifies. Not only will their
crops be cut off, but their ranks will be decimated by bar-
renness, miscarriage, and bereavement:

> Ephraim's glory shall fly away like a bird —
>   no birth, no pregnancy, no conception!
> Even if they bring up children,
>   I will bereave them till none is left.
>   (9:11-12)

> Give them, O Lord —
>   what wilt thou give?
> Give them a miscarrying womb
>   and dry breasts.
>   (9:14; cf. 13:16)

The sovereignty of God in judgment shows up clearly
in Hosea's repeated announcements that foreign alliances
cannot stay the execution of God's plan. Neither Assyria
nor Egypt is a match for him when he decides that what
Israel has failed to learn in mercy they must learn in wrath
(5:9-14; 8:8-13). Far from saving Israel from destruction,
the neighboring nations will be the means used by God to
bring it about (10:14-15; 11:5-7). Invasion will lead to exile,
as the Israelites who have fed to the full on their own soil
are chastened by deprivation in a hostile land.

In other words God, who holds nature and history in his
hand, will use both as whips to drive his people to their
knees. He will not allow them to depend either on allies
or on their own kings, for whom they had begged God so

persistently in the early days of their history (13:9-11). He knows that from a perspective of desolation they will see themselves as they really are and turn to him for mercy.

A point to remember is that God bears the full brunt of responsibility for his activities in nature and in history. What we would call natural disaster or historical coincidence, the Bible sees as God's acts of judgment or grace. We may not understand all that he is doing, but we cannot doubt that in his own wisdom and power he is impelling the course of life to its divinely decreed destination.

God takes the initiative in forgiveness and restoration to fellowship. We have already commented on the moving passage (2:14ff.) where God, who has been forgotten by the Israelites, pledges himself to reach out to Israel, allure her and draw her to himself. This scene of restoration culminates in a grand covenant ceremony which all of nature is summoned to witness (2:21-23). In striking poetic personification, the message of God's forgiveness is sounded from heaven to earth and then relayed to the crops (which God had withheld) and finally to the people of Israel.

In a word-play on the names of the children, God heralds a new day of acceptance and fellowship for Israel. In chapter one Jezreel symbolizes God's scattering in judgment (1:4-5); in chapter two it speaks of God's replanting in restoration (2:22-23). This pun is possible because in Hebrew Jezreel means both "God will scatter" and "God will sow." Pity will be shown to Lo-ruhamah (not-pitied), and Lo-ammi (not-my-people) will regain his place in God's favor.

God's grace operating through his judgment prepared the people for a new and greater relationship — a relationship brought to fulfillment in the New Testament. This hopeful

strain from Hosea is echoed in the stirring words of Peter:
"Once you were no people but now you are God's people;
once you had not received mercy but now you have received
mercy" (I Peter 2:10).

Though much of the book is freighted with threats of
judgment, Hosea's final word is a pledge of forgiveness and
a promise of blessing:

> I will heal their faithlessness;
>   I will love them freely,
>   for my anger has turned from them.
>   (14:4)
>
>   . . . . . .
> They shall return and dwell beneath my shadow,
>   they shall flourish as a garden;
> they shall blossom as the vine,
>   their fragrance shall be like the wine of Lebanon.
>   (14:7)

Israel deserved to receive full judgment. But God, in faithfulness to his covenant made at the Exodus, and out of compassion for those whom he has chosen, holds open the door
of forgiveness. And even more, he urges, pleads, and even
threatens in order to reunite the covenant family. At times
when he is far from their thoughts, they stand in the center
of his. He even supplies the words of repentance with which
they can acknowledge their guilt and seek his face (Hosea
5:15–6:3; 14:2-3).

In this book and in all of Scripture, the divine initiative
is seen as primary. In creation and throughout the annals
of history, God plays the stellar role. In the virgin birth
and at the cross, God has taken the divine initiative in salvation. In the second coming of Christ, the final judgment,

and the new heaven and earth, God takes full responsibility for the course of events.

God, in ways that we cannot understand, is always in control of the whole range of reality. God has righteous purposes toward which he is ever moving, and he insists that those who want to be related to him as responsible servants move toward these goals with him. However discordant the polyphony of human events may sound to our ears, the universe is tuned to sing his praise, and the final arrangement will be one of perfect harmony.

God Maintains His Righteousness

There is a great deal of emphasis in Hosea upon right standards of conduct and attitude. The people were being judged because they had failed to conform to the standards God had set, and there is no suggestion that at any point God was going to trim these standards. There is no hint that because man cannot jump high enough to clear the bar of His righteousness, God is going to lower it.

This is a tremendously important concept in an age which is rather sentimental in its view of God. Nowhere does this show up more clearly· than in some of the popular songs which have a religious tone. We find so often that the "man upstairs" in these songs bears little or no resemblance to the God of Scripture. Some of our gospel songs are little better; they are doggerel expressions of some immature, wishful thinking. We have to come back to the prophets, back to the God and Father of Jesus Christ, to see a God who is unsullied in his righteousness and who, if he were not, would cease to be God.

In Hosea's every denunciation of sin, in his every threat

of judgment, in his every call to repentance, there rings the righteousness of God. But interwoven with the themes of divine initiative and divine righteousness there is the recurring strain of divine grace.

God Balances Judgment with Mercy

There is within the personality of God a balance of his righteousness and his forgiving love, of his wrath and his mercy. Forgiveness as *God* forgives and redemption as *God* redeems do not mean an ignoring or glossing over of the human predicament. God, in providing the means of our salvation, in building the bridge by which we can come back to him, does not overlook sin. He faces it, he judges it, he deals with it directly.

We know that mercy and judgment are simultaneously present in the character of God because we see them in the activity of God. As Hosea puts it, "for he has torn, that he may heal us; he has stricken, and he will bind us up" (6:1). God's judgment is related to his forgiveness and his wrath to his love, though the relationship is not always clear to us. God is not erratic or inconsistent, sometimes acting one way and sometimes another, but works all things together for good as he sees it.

In God the opposing elements hate (of sin) and love (for man) are completely bound together. "I will love them no more," God says (9:15), and then, "I will love them freely" (14:4). His intense hatred of sin, free from spite and rancor, causes God to act as though he does not love, and yet this very act of withholding his love is an expression of his greater love.

And so God can say,

How can I give you up, O Ephraim!
How can I hand you over, O Israel!
. . . . .
My heart recoils within me,
my compassion grows warm and tender.
I will not execute my fierce anger. . . .
(11:8-9)

His fierce anger is there; he doesn't disguise it. There is a warmth of compassion and a fierceness of anger that are operating simultaneously and in harmony within the personality of God. "For I am God," he says, "and not man, the Holy One in your midst, and I will not come to destroy" (11:9). Only God loves completely enough and purely enough to be able to judge with absolute objectivity.

This perfect union of wrath and love in God's person is hard for us to grasp because it is so foreign to our natures. For this reason we need to learn about our family relationships from him. The more purely we love our children, the more objectively we will be able to judge their actions and bring discipline that is appropriate to the offense. We parents seem to alternate between weak or flabby discipline and undue harshness with our children. Often we try to compensate for our harsh treatment by taking them places or placating them with gifts. Frequent indecision, inconsistency, and flights of temper indicate a lack of security in our love; they are telling testimonies to the toll that sin takes on our ability to act in wisdom and maturity toward our own.

Because we are not really free, because selfishness throttles our efforts to relate not only to our families but to those in our school or work situations, it is difficult for us to achieve a proper balance of love and forgiveness with righteousness and discipline in dealing with these emotion-charged situations. As we fail to face up to these feelings of hostility or inadequacy we are apt to go to the extremes of rashness or over-permissiveness. Once they have been identified, only grace — that unearned love of God — and wisdom, which he gives to all who ask, can rescue us from the destructive forces of sin.

Hosea, like the book of Job, underscores *the freedom of God,* the right of God to be God. God's love and God's grace, in other words, can never be presumed upon. This was the fatal mistake of the Israelites. They naively assumed that they were exempt from judgment because of their special claim upon God's favor. Neither they nor we can sin and get away with it. We can count on God's love and forgiveness, but we cannot presume upon them. Our part is to trust God by obeying him as fully as we can, not to test him by straying as far as we dare. Any attempt we make to test or manipulate God shows that we have not recognized him as the Holy One of Israel.

Whenever we talk about the freedom of God, we must at the same time stress *the dependability of God.* The one who comes unto him he will not cast out. Those who hunger and thirst after righteousness will be filled. If any man lack wisdom, let him ask of God.

Freedom and dependability work in harmony within the nature of God in a way that is difficult for human beings to grasp. The reason for this difficulty is that freedom and responsibility, freedom and dependability, freedom and steadfastness are often in opposition to each other within our own personalities.

Most men would like to have more freedom to come and go without rigid schedules at home or at work. But if we press this desire for flexibility, we create upsetting situations. Our chances for domestic tranquility and economic prosperity are better if we can maintain a regular schedule. So we find ourselves as inept jugglers trying to keep responsibility, dependability, and steadfastness in balance with a feeling of freedom.

God alone maintains this perfect balance. He is not fettered by creaturely or sinful limitations. His dependability means, among other things, that he is working even when we are unaware of it. God's activity in our lives, in society, in history, does not depend upon our recognition of it.

Christ once said to some of the Jews, "My Father is working still, and I am working" (John 5:17). In effect he was saying, "He rested on the seventh day after creation and he has not rested since." He is actively involved in all of life; he is working in ways that we do not understand and in places that we do not know about, in mysteries that we cannot fathom and in people that we might not suspect of being his instruments. He does not leave the stage of history for periods of time and then re-enter. He is involved in the processes of reality, and his dependability means that he is unchanging and ever righteous, however relative our standards may be.

There is a steadfastness about God in the midst of his freedom so that when we call, he hears; when we cry, he answers. His response is not always understood by us; he does not always answer as we want him to, but it is in godly freedom that he ministers to our needs. His attitude toward us does not necessarily depend on our attitude toward him.

He is God to us in the way that he sees fit, not in the way that we deem right.

Hosea did not volunteer for the kind of suffering that came his way. He did not compile a list and say, "I want these experiences." God was God to Hosea, but he was God to Hosea on His own terms.

Responsible, available, steadfast; at the same time free to do what he wants to do in the light of his greater knowledge and his greater love, to lead men in ways they do not understand in order to make them what he wants them to be. This is Hosea's God — and ours.

Chapter Six

THE QUEST FOR THE KNOWLEDGE OF GOD

Let us know, let us press on to know the Lord. . . .
(Hosea 6:3)

It is the wonder of the book of Hosea — and of the whole Bible — that God seeks fellowship with man. He made man capable of this relationship in the beginning and continued to pursue him even when man rebelled and refused to respond to His quest. He entered into a gracious contract with Israel and persevered in his love despite Israel's failure to live up to the terms of the contract.

Hosea's attempts to bring the Israelites to their senses and to rekindle within their hearts love for God and his law consisted, for the most part, in pointing up their need for *the knowledge of God.*

Although the knowledge of God was an intellectual concept for the Hebrews, it was not merely theoretical. The Old Testament makes no distinction between theory and practice, between idea and fact, or between thought and action. We talk about theories that do not work, about plans that miscarry, about advice that falls flat. And we say to ourselves as we brush our hands and move away from the wreck of some situation that we have created or contributed to, "It was a good plan but it didn't work."

81

An Israelite could never make that distinction. The only way he knew a good plan was that it worked. The only way he knew that a person was wise was that this person acted in wisdom. The only way he knew that there was true knowledge was that this knowledge was productive in everyday experience.

What Hosea was saying when he talked about "the knowledge of God" was not that the Israelites should obtain more information about God. The Israelites were aware of God's guiding hand in their history; they knew something of his character, for they extolled his praises and declared his attributes in their public worship. But they did not know him. They recited their creeds; they listened to the reading of the Scriptures; they carried out the details of the Biblical feasts with meticulous care; but they did not know the Lord. They had an abundant store of knowledge *about* God, but they were destitute in their knowledge *of* God.

Hosea's indictment of Israel charges:

> There is no faithfulness or kindness,
> > and no *knowledge of God* in the land.
> > > (4:1)

God's holy requirements are set forth:

> For I desire steadfast love and not sacrifice,
> > the *knowledge of God,* rather than burnt
> > offerings.
> > > (6:6)

The Knowledge of God Involves Obedience

A closer look at these theme passages brings to view the basic elements of this concept. The Lord declares in his controversy with Israel (4:1-2) that there is no knowledge of God in the land; instead, there is swearing, lying, killing, stealing, committing adultery. They break all bonds and murder follows murder. The statement that there is no knowledge of God is followed immediately by a statement that the law is being shattered into small pieces by the disobedient Israelites. This indicates that one factor involved in the knowledge of God is obedience to the law of God. And where there is disobedience, there is no true knowledge of God.

This is confirmed in 4:6 where the prophet addresses himself particularly to the priests, who failed in their responsibility to give to the people religious leadership and instruction in the law:

> My people are destroyed for lack of knowledge;
> because you have rejected knowledge,
> I reject you from being a priest to me.
> And since you have forgotten the law of your God,
> I also will forget your children.

Notice the Hebrew parallelism in which the last part of the verse actually comments on the first part, indicating that the priestly line will be broken off. The forgetting of the law is clear evidence that the priests have rejected the knowledge of God.

God makes it plain that Israel's future relationship with him will have to be different when the remarriage takes place:

> I will betroth you to me in *righteousness* and in *justice*, in *steadfast love,* and in *mercy.* I will betroth you to me in *faithfulness;* and you shall know the Lord.
>
> (2:19-20)

The Hebrew word translated "in" means here "in exchange for" or "for the price of." It is used in II Samuel 3:14, where David betrothed Michal "at the price of" a hundred foreskins of the Philistines; so God asks a high price of the Israelites: a complete about-face. Their wickedness will be replaced by righteousness; their injustice and oppression of the poor will give way to justice, steadfast love, and mercy; their spiritual infidelity will be transformed into faithfulness to the one true God.

In other words, God will require of Israel obedience to the terms of the covenant: *righteousness* means conformity to God's standards; *justice* denotes a safeguarding of the rights of all citizens; *steadfast love* speaks of extending to others the same kind of constant and gracious concern that God had extended to Israel; *mercy* involves a particular interest in the problems and needs of the less privileged members of the community; *faithfulness* is constant and unswerving dependability and devotion. These requirements are summed up in the final clause: "and you shall know the Lord." To know God is to live in accordance with his standards.

Repentance Is Prerequisite to the Knowledge of God

Failure to obey had alienated the unrepentant Israelites from God. This is what God says about them:

> I know Ephraim,
> and Israel is not hid from me;
> for now, O Ephraim, you have played the harlot,
> Israel is defiled.
> Their deeds do not permit them
> to return to their God.
> For the spirit of harlotry is within them,
> and they know not the Lord.
>
> (5:3-4)

Fellowship had been broken. They had wandered off into

unbridled worship of the pagan gods, particularly the various forms of Baal.

Now the term "return to their God" implies, in Old Testament language, repentance. Almost any time the words "turn" or "return" occur, the idea of repentance can be substituted. What God was saying was that they had not repented so as to restore the right relationship, so as to enter into fullness of fellowship; they did not know the Lord, they were not in fellowship with him.

Repentance is at times expressed in terms of seeking. The time is foretold (3:5) when the children of Israel will "return and *seek*" the Lord. Repentance is again implicit in 5:15 where God insists that they "acknowledge their guilt and *seek* my face" before complete reunion can take place. The idea of seeking as a condition of salvation is evident in Hosea's challenge to Israel:

> Sow for yourselves righteousness,
>   reap the fruit of steadfast love;
>   break up your fallow ground,
> for it is time to *seek* the Lord,
>   that he may come and rain salvation upon you.
>   (10:12)

We should bear in mind that the terms "seek the Lord" or "seek my face" refer not so much to the private devotion of the individual as to the public confession of the congregation. Hosea's call was for the members of the Israelite community to assemble, to acknowledge their corporate guilt and to reaffirm their loyalty to the covenant way. The acid test of their sincerity was not just the intensity of their repentance but the integrity of their conduct. Not merely zeal but love was to be the fruit of their repentance.

Repentance is our way of acknowledging not only that we have been wrong but that God is right. It brings us face to face with our failure to love and serve him as we should. There is no substitute for it and no way to by-pass it in our relationship to God. A glib attitude toward repentance is a sure sign that one has missed the meaning of the holiness of God. As obedience is prerequisite to knowing God, so repentance is demanded when we have failed to obey. Fellowship is conditional, requiring both obedience and repentance, because we can have fellowship with God only on his terms. We cannot write the rules. God says, "This is my requirement, that you recognize my lordship, that you yield to me in repentance, obedience and love, and then you can have fellowship with me."

God's terms are made explicit in Hosea's prophecy. After describing the direst kind of judgment in which he promises to ravage Ephraim and Judah like a lion (5:14), God pictures himself retiring and waiting for Israel to take stock of his guilt and seek His forgiveness (5:15). He even gives them the call to repentance which they will have to utter:

> Come, let us return to the Lord;
> for he has torn, that he may heal us;
> he has stricken, and he will bind us up.
> After two days he will revive us;
> on the third day he will raise us up,
> that we may live before him.
> Let us know, let us press on to know the Lord;
> his going forth is sure as the dawn;
> he will come to us as the showers,
> as the spring rains that water the earth.
> (6:1-3; cf. 14:1-3)

There may have been times in Israel when certain groups tried to snap the chains of idolatry and return to their rightful Master. The preaching of Amos may well have evoked such a response. But apparently the cost was too great. Whatever show of repentance and devotion Israel could muster was so temporary that God laments his people's fickleness and compares their love to dew which disappears by mid-morning (6:4).

The Knowledge of God Results in Fellowship

The idea of fellowship which has the warmth and intimacy of a love relationship is brought out in one of Hosea's most memorable passages:

> Therefore, behold, I will allure her,
>> and bring her into the wilderness,
>> and speak tenderly to her.
>
> . . . . .
>
> And there she shall answer as in the days of her
>> youth,
>> as at the time when she came out of the land
>> of Egypt.
> And in that day, says the Lord, you will call me, "My
> husband," and no longer will you call me, "My Baal."
>
> . . . . .
>
> I will betroth you to me in faithfulness; and you shall
> know the Lord.
>
> (2:14-16, 20)

This whole passage rings with overtones of love. God courts Israel and she responds to his wooing. Betrothal follows and then marriage, a marriage expressed in terms of utmost intimacy: "You shall know the Lord." Such knowledge involves a pledge of deepest loyalty, a willingness to risk all else for the sake of this relationship, a total investment of Israel in the way and will of her divine husband. This loyalty is to be reflected in the name by which Israel addresses

God. "My Baal" in Hebrew means "my lord" and was a
standard way in which Israelite wives addressed their husbands. Because the word "Baal" had idolatrous overtones,
God forbade Israel to refer to him by it and substituted a
term which could have no connection with Baal-worship —
"My husband" (literally "my man").

As this change of name suggests, fellowship with God
has an exclusive side to it. Our relationship to him has to
be different from our relationship to anyone else. For this
reason marriage is a good illustration of it. As wife and husband depend directly on each other for certain needs, so
fellowship with God means that Israel must look to him
for her protection and sustenance while God looks to Israel
to spread the knowledge of him among the nations.

It is with this in mind that Hosea lashes out at the
entangling alliances which in Israel became substitutes for
trust in God. Not only Baal-worship but dependence on
foreign nations became a chief target of the prophet's at-
tack (5:13; 7:9-13; 8:9-10). The futility of Israel's frantic
search for aid and comfort apart from God is nowhere made
clearer than in 12:1:

> Ephraim herds the wind,
>   and pursues the east wind all day long;
> they multiply falsehood and violence;
>   they make a bargain with Assyria,
>   and oil is carried to Egypt.

True fellowship with God also precluded Israel's dependence on military might. Fortified cities, crack chariotry,
and warriors armed to the teeth could not substitute for
wholehearted reliance on God (8:14; 10:13). Living by the
sword meant ultimately perishing by the sword (10:14, 15).

Toward the close of the book Hosea sums up what God expects of those who know him:

> Return, O Israel, to the Lord your God,
>> for you have stumbled because of your iniquity.
>
> Take with you words
>> and return to the Lord;
>
> say to him,
>> "Take away all iniquity;
>
> accept that which is good
>> and we will render
>> the fruit of our lips.
>
> Assyria shall not save us,
>> we will not ride upon horses;
>
> and we will say no more, 'Our God,'
>> to the work of our hands.
>
> In thee the orphan finds mercy."
>
> (14:1-3)

God himself stipulates the terms by which Israel will find full restoration: true repentance in which contrition takes the place of sacrifice; dependence upon him, not foreign alliances or military might; rejection of all idolatrous patterns of worship; acceptance of the meaning of his mercy.

These false allegiances, to which Israel was so prone, become all the more tragic when viewed in the light of the Exodus (9:10; 11:1-3; 13:4-8). There God had proved beyond a doubt his ability to meet their needs. He had whipped the hosts of Pharaoh into submission and had tamed the hostile forces of the sea and wilderness in delivering his people from bondage. He had given spiritual leadership through Moses and the prophets (12:10, 13). Thus equipped and provided for, Israel was commanded to keep herself free from lesser loyalties and to enjoy her fellowship with

God — to know him and him alone in an intimacy akin to marriage.

This concept of the knowledge of God lays hold of man at the center of his being, touching the whole person. This is not a matter of knowing right propositions about God. Our orthodoxy can never be substituted for the knowledge of God. We can be orthodox and be lost. We can have most of our doctrines straight and still be living as rebels within, and not know God. For us, as for the Israelites, knowing God includes not only right ideas but a right relationship which judges our self-centeredness and sets us free to live in love.

The New Testament picks up this theme and plays it in even clearer tones. In the midst of a denunciation that Christ brings upon Chorazin and Bethsaida, he utters a brief but important prayer:

> I thank thee, Father, Lord of heaven and earth, that thou hast hidden these things from the wise and understanding and revealed them to babes; yea, Father, for such was thy gracious will. All things have been delivered to me by my Father; and no one knows the Son except the Father, and no one knows the Father except the Son and any one to whom the Son chooses to reveal him.
>
> (Matthew 11:25-27)

The intimate, exclusive kinship between the Father and the Son is expressed in terms of *knowing*. This knowledge is available only in personal encounter. That is why true knowledge of God comes only through Christ, in whom God has revealed himself to us. Christ goes on to make clear that the yoke (a figure used in Hosea 10:11 and 11:4) of total commitment is the condition for such knowledge:

> Come to me, all who labor and are heavy-laden, and I will give you rest. Take my yoke upon you, and learn from me; for I am gentle and lowly in heart, and you will find rest for your souls. For my yoke is easy, and my burden is light.
>
> (Matthew 11:28-30)

Again, in his high-priestly prayer, Jesus says:

> And this is eternal life, that they know thee the only true God, and Jesus Christ whom thou hast sent.
>
> (John 17:3)

Christ is drawing again on the background of the concept of knowing God that Hosea lines out for us — repentance, obedience, and love.

The connection between knowing God, obeying God, and loving God is emphasized again in I John 2:3-6:

> And by this we may be sure that we know him, if we keep his commandments. He who says "I know him" but disobeys his commandments is a liar, and the truth is not in him; but whoever keeps his word, in him truly love for God is perfected. By this we may be sure that we are in him: he who says he abides in him ought to walk in the same way in which he walked.

One of the many terms in Scripture that describe our relationship to God is *fear*. To fear the Lord is equivalent in the Psalms and wisdom literature (such as Job and Proverbs) to the prophetic concept of knowing God. This does not mean that we quake in our boots when we think about God. This means that we take his lordship seriously, that we acknowledge his sovereignty over every area of life, and that we willingly accept his direction.

Trust is another term used in speaking of our relationship to God. It implies a great deal more than merely believing in God. There is a modern cult of having faith in faith, a "keep your chin up" kind of religion. The object of this faith is not always stressed; it is just a matter of having a vague confidence in some unidentified "supreme being."

Now when the Bible talks about believing in God, or believing God, or trusting God, it means that we put our whole weight upon him. It means that we stake all that we have and all that we are on the reality of what God is. This is not merely an assent to an intellectual proposition that God exists. It is taking his existence with the kind of seriousness that translates faith into action.

It becomes apparent, then, that these various terms present slightly different facets of the basic concept of knowing God. This is why John can talk about *trusting* God, Hosea and Jesus can talk about *knowing* God. Paul talks about *having faith,* and the wisdom writers in the Old Testament talk about *fearing* God. There is in each expression the same wholehearted commitment to what God is. There is the same recognition of his sovereignty and of the fact that we live abundant and fruitful lives only as we live in total dependence upon him.

This is what Hosea meant when he implored Israel to know God and warned that lack of knowledge would bring destruction. This is what Jesus meant when he said that to know him is to find life indeed.

Chapter Seven

THE INWARDNESS OF TRUE RELIGION

For I desire steadfast love and not sacrifice,
the knowledge of God, rather than burnt
offerings.

(Hosea 6:6)

In this chapter we face one of the vexing problems of
the Old Testament. How is it that the God who ordained
Israel's formal worship in the tabernacle and temple and
gave detailed directions for the feasts and sacrifices actually
seems to reject the sacred rites which he instituted? Not
only Hosea but many of the great prophets — Amos, Isaiah,
Micah, Jeremiah — speak out against the religious activities
as though they should have been abandoned altogether by
the people.

"Love, not sacrifice," is God's way according to Hosea
(6:6). Yet in the days of Moses God ordained sacrifice and
burnt offerings as part of the religious life of Israel.

Had God changed his program? Was there a contradic-
tion involved in the Biblical revelation? Was Moses incor-
rect in instituting the sacrificial system or was Hosea wrong
in criticizing it as he did? How do we reconcile what seem
to be contradictory emphases?

Part of the explanation is that the prophets often put

across their message by *overstatement,* a characteristic Hebrew method of expression. The prophets would say, for example, when one thing is a little better than another, that this is "good" and that is "no good."

This is clearly seen in the book of Malachi (1:2-3) where God says, "Yet I have loved Jacob, but I have hated Esau." Here he is using black and white terms, love — hate. But if we understand the context of the passage and the nature of Hebrew language, we realize that God is saying, "I have *preferred* Jacob to Esau. I have given him a priority in my program of election."

Similarly, when God says, "I desire steadfast love and not sacrifice" in typical Hebrew idiom, he is saying, "I desire steadfast love *more* than sacrifice." The second line bears this out: "the knowledge of God rather than burnt offerings," or "the knowledge of God *more* than burnt offerings." And so in making this contrast, he is not rejecting sacrifice completely but stressing inward attitude more than outward act.

Inward attitude and outward act — both were important to the faith of Israel. Our task in this chapter is to see the role of each and the connection between them.

The Purpose of the Cultus

As we look at the external side of Israel's faith, the word cult — or cultus — will be used. "Cult," as we use it popularly, usually refers to one of the sects on the backwaters of Christianity, a group that would be considered heretical. But when the word "cult" or "cultus" is used in referring to the religion of Israel, it means the formal, external side of Israel's religious life: the priesthood, the sacrifices, the tabernacle or temple, the feasts, the fasts, and all of the regulations that have to do with the formal worship of the Israelite community.

What part had God intended the formal worship to play in the lives of the people? It was to have been a regular reminder of their dependence upon him and their commitment to the covenant which he had made with them.

The religion of Israel touched all three tenses: past, present, and future. One basic purpose of the feasts, which were the formal celebrations of Israel's covenant faith, was to remind the people of the acts of God in the *past*. These festivities most often commemorated the Israelites' deliverance from Egypt. It was this Exodus experience that lay at the heart of Israel's faith.

Some of the Psalms were written specifically for use in the religious life of the people to celebrate what God had done in the past, in the lives of the patriarchs and in the Exodus. The overtones of the past can be heard, for example, in Psalm 105:

> He is mindful of his covenant for ever,
>> of the word that he commanded, for a thousand
>>> generations,
> the covenant which he made with Abraham,
>> his sworn promise to Isaac,
> which he confirmed to Jacob as a statute,
>> to Israel as an everlasting covenant,
> saying, "To you I will give the land of Canaan
>> as your portion for an inheritance."
>>> (Psalm 105:8-11)

The Psalmist is drawing heavily on the Genesis stories of Abraham, Isaac, and Jacob. As the Psalm continues it becomes clear that it is a canticle of praise to God, the divine Overseer, a joyous recounting of Israel's step-at-a-time progression from Egypt to Canaan, the promised land.

One can almost hear the congregation at the Feast of Tabernacles in the autumn, or Passover in the spring, celebrating the past deliverance by joining in this recitation of the mighty acts of God:

> Then he led forth Israel with silver and gold,
>> and there was none among his tribes who stumbled.
> Egypt was glad when they departed,
>> for dread of them had fallen upon it.
>
> . . . . .
>
> So he led forth his people with joy,
>> his chosen ones with singing.
>> (Psalm 105:37, 38, 43)

The cultus, the official public worship, was a formal way of assuring that the people of Israel would continue to be conscious of their past, that they would not view themselves as people without heritage or destiny. It was a forceful reminder that they, the Israelites of Hosea's day, were the latest links in a chain which stretched back to Abraham, and that God had been forging link after link for his holy purposes.

The *present* aspect of the public worship in Israel was to recreate, to make personal, to help the people appropriate these acts of God. There is a sense in which all of us identify with our past and dedicate ourselves to the ideals for which earlier patriots fought and died. On the Fourth of July we freedom-loving Americans remember the minutemen, recapture a bit of the spirit of '76, and say to ourselves, "In a sense, I was there." In much the same way, at Passover an Israelite would look at his past, recall the Exodus, and say, "I was there." In doing so he would renew his commitment to obey the law of God. For the privilege of redemption brought with it the obligation of obedience.

Memory of redemption was also a call to compassion. The Israelites had known the sting of suffering, the despair of slavery, and the dejection of exile. Part of their covenant duty was to be concerned for those in similar situations (Exodus 22:21).

Past was linked to present as they celebrated Passover, Tabernacles, and other holy days. In these festivities the Israelites reaffirmed God's redemptive activity in their lives, acknowledged his sovereignty over *now* as well as *then,* and appropriated his forgiveness through their sacrifices and offerings.

Just before the Israelites crossed over Jordan into Canaan, Moses had outlined the procedure for these thanksgiving services, as well as the spoken response of the Israelites. This response (Deuteronomy 26:5-15) was much like an Apostles' Creed and contained: (1) A rehearsal of past events: "A wandering Aramean was my father; and he went down into Egypt and sojourned there...he became a nation great, mighty, and populous. And the Egyptians...laid upon us hard bondage...and the Lord brought us out of Egypt...and gave us...a land flowing with milk and honey." (2) An offering of the first fruits of the harvest as a token of dedication and vicarious involvement in the redemption from bondage: "And behold, now I bring the first of the fruit of the ground, which thou, O Lord, hast given me." (3) A closing invocation of God's blessing on the people of Israel: "Look down from thy holy habitation...and bless thy people Israel and the ground which thou hast given us...a land flowing with milk and honey."

Finally, the cultus looked to the *future* for a grand climax to these mighty acts of God. The Exodus experience was a guarantee that God would break into history in the future and bring a new day. Isaiah talked about a new Exodus (Isaiah 43:15ff.) and Jeremiah promised that the old covenant graven in stone at Sinai would be replaced by a new covenant etched in the hearts of the Israelites (Jeremiah 31:31).

Thus the old became the pattern for the new. As the Israelites of Hosea's time looked back to the Exodus experience, celebrated the acts of God, appropriated the inspiration of those acts, and dedicated themselves anew to God, they looked forward to a time when full deliverance would come. God, who had led the way in the Exodus experience, once again would break into history in this same dramatic fashion and the earth would come to the full knowledge of him.

The Failure of the Cultus

But the Israelites failed to understand the true meaning of the cult and gave it a pagan turn which Hosea had to oppose. Their moral and spiritual lives were not being governed by the covenant, but by Canaanite custom: Baal was getting credit for the good gifts of God, and cultic rites were separating the people from the covenant relationship.

Nor were they able to look forward to the future, because they were involved in nature-worship, which, by definition, knows no future. The purpose of nature-worship was not to celebrate the acts of God in history but by magical practices and cultic formulas to make sure that in the spring the fruit trees would blossom and the ewes would drop their lambs.

Nature-worship looks for a continuous repetition of the

same cycle, and so never moves anywhere; it has no real beginning or end. It was distinctive of Israel's faith that it looked back, that it saw the present in terms of the past, and that it looked ahead and saw the present in terms of the future. This is quite a different thing from a religion grounded in nature, where the cycles of the sun and the seasons turn with wearisome monotony.

It becomes apparent that this corruption of Israel's worship was not merely a matter of the infiltration of a few pagan practices. It was a completely different outlook on reality. Was God really Lord of history, beginning a program at creation and carrying it through to its fulfillment? Or was life an endless round in which Baal spun the wheel?

We have already seen (chapter three) the excesses to which Israelites went when they missed the meaning of the cultus. Drunkenness, cult prostitution, magical practices, idolatry, masochism, ruthless oppression of the underprivileged, and naive dependence upon foreign powers — these were the alarming symptoms of a religious devotion turned sick.

In contrast to the time-honored Hebrew tradition of prayer, the Israelites were engaging in ritualistic lamentation:

> They do not cry to me from the heart,
>   but they wail upon their beds. . . .
> (7:14)

The many examples of Hebrew prayers in Scripture indicate that they were quite intelligible and spoken in straightforward fashion. The Hebrews recognized their relation to God, their dependence upon him; they stated their case, their needs; they made their petitions known and asked God to minister to these needs and requests. And often, particularly in the Psalms, they praised him in advance for the answer.

The error of Israel's life was compounded by the fact that the formality of their religion was completely divorced from the quality of their living. They had a ritualistic religion without an ethical content. They went through ceremonies perfunctorily and without inner involvement.

Israel's plight was made more acute by the fact that the priests, whose task it was to instruct the people in the meaning of their worship, had themselves forgotten God's law. Instead of pointing the people to God, they were actually "greedy for their iniquity" (4:8). Worship had been degraded by them to a commercial enterprise offering possibilities of great gain through exploitation. The holy days and festivals proved exceedingly profitable as the priests took their cut of the sacrifices and offerings of the congregation. This was neither the first nor the last time that a house of prayer became a den of thieves.

Because of the joint guilt of people and priests in this offense against God, a joint sentence was passed:

> And it shall be like people, like priest;
> I will punish them for their ways,
> and requite them for their deeds.
> (4:9)

The total futility of Israel's perverted worship was called to the people's attention by a biting word-play. Hosea refers to Beth-el, "House of God," the sacred site of Jacob's encounter with God (Genesis 28:10-17; Hosea 12:4) as Beth-aven, "House of Nothing" or "House of Emptiness" (4:15; 10:5, 8). The majesty of God's presence had been traded for the uselessness of a golden calf.

Here was tragedy indeed. The cultus, which God had provided as a reminder of his grace and a means of fellowship with him, had become a barrier to devotion when its purposes were obscured. The priesthood, appointed by God and carefully regulated by his statutes, not only had failed to stem the tide of impiety but had contributed to it. In the face of this failure Hosea voiced a threat and a plea. He promised the destruction of the shrines and altars where worship had become so corrupted that men were kissing calves (13:2; 10:1, 2, 8; 12:11). He pleaded for a change of heart, a conversion in which hollow ritual would be transformed into a covenant faith that would manifest itself in righteousness and justice (10:12).

Hosea and the New Testament

When Christ delivered the Sermon on the Mount, he rephrased the law in terms of this prophetic emphasis on the inwardness of true religion. He held that men are as responsible for their thoughts as for their deeds. Hatred and murder, lust and adultery are cut from the same cloth. It is the attitude within that counts: the prayer in the closet, not in the market place; the alms given in secret, not heralded with the trumpet blast (Matthew 5:21—6:4).

In stressing thoughts, feelings, and motives, Christ was taking the Jewish religion, which had been shunted onto a siding of legalism, back onto the main track of prophetic emphasis on personal righteousness. At least twice in the New Testament the Lord showed his spiritual kinship with Hosea by quoting, "I desire mercy and not sacrifice" (Matthew 9:13; 12:7). He pointed out God's requirements not as an innovator, but as a reformer; not as one who was heralding something new so much as one who was bringing the people back to where they should have been.

Christ had come to give the law and the prophets their full meaning, to bring the fullness of his own example to the sketchiness of their precepts, not because these precepts were wrong, but because they were subject to wrong interpretation:

> Think not that I have come to abolish the law and the prophets; I have come not to abolish them but to fulfil them.
>
> (Matthew 5:17)

Jesus Christ came not only to die as redeemer, but to live as an example of Spirit-guided obedience, to set a pattern for the kind of discipleship to which he himself calls us. And to jog the consciences of the Pharisees, Christ reached back to the prophets like Hosea and said, in effect, "You have missed the point. Life does not consist of a punctilious keeping of ceremonial requirements, of a legalistic paying of the tithe, of a rigid regulating of conduct as to diet and dress. You must come to know God in this new relationship of inner obedience and love of which Hosea spoke, and then you will know what life is all about."

And so Hosea, with his emphases on the inwardness of true religion, on forgiveness and fellowship, on obedience and discipleship, was actually blazing the trail along which Christ himself walked and became one of those voices in the wilderness helping to prepare the way of the Lord.

What has been said about the purpose of the cultus of Israel could be applied to Christian worship, particularly to the tangible expression of it in the Lord's Supper. There is an element of the past in it. We look back to the cross, realizing that what was done there was sufficient for all time and need never be repeated. In the present we appropriate the strength of Christ's atonement. We ask forgiveness, saying, in effect, "I, too, was crucified with Christ," as though we had actually been there. Thus the past becomes contemporary in the Communion. Then we look ahead as Paul did when he said, "For as often as you eat this bread and drink this cup you proclaim the Lord's death until he comes" (I Corinthians 11:26).

There is no religious life that does not take some external form. This is just the way we are as people. We want something tangible, we want structure for our religious experience. Those of us who are of a less formal church tradition tend to look down on liturgy or ritual, and yet we have our own ceremonial structure. We meet to worship at a certain time on the same day of each week, in buildings which have organs and certain kinds of glass. This is structure. The order of worship is prescribed in bulletins. More structure. But without this form to our worship services, we would be completely insecure, with no idea of where to begin, how to proceed, or when to end.

This structure is grounded in Scripture. God gave it in the Old Testament in a more concrete and detailed fashion; he reaffirmed it in the New Testament in Baptism and the Lord's Supper. In appointing deacons and designating the Lord's day as the chief day of worship, the early Church was building a framework for itself.

Those who are accustomed to a less formal church service should be most tolerant of those whose worship is steeped in liturgy. Informality sometimes turns church meetings into club meetings. In striving to create a friendly, folksy atmosphere, ministers with strong pulpit personalities often assume star-performer roles that put worship of God on the periphery instead of at the heart of the service.

The psalms of the Old Testament were vibrant hymns of praise to a mighty, redeeming God; our "Christian" music too often includes sacred themes couched in sentimental parodies that have little to do with either the true nature of God or the reality of human experience. It is one thing to be informal; it is another to treat redemptive truths tritely. It is one thing to express our Christian faith in personal terms; it is another to resort to gospel jingles or syrupy ballads which smack of sensuality, if not sexuality.

Conversely, churches in which liturgy and ritual are the dominant elements of the service are subject to dangers of quite another sort. It is possible to become so spiritually lulled by the beauty and symmetry of the liturgy, by the sameness of the services, that it is difficult to establish a warm personal contact with God. When the vital ministry of the Holy Spirit departs, a dead and lifeless shell is all that remains.

Pagan practices within our structured church life often take the form of gimmicks or tricks which we would substitute for the power of the Holy Spirit. Soul-winning statistics, blatant advertising, competitions and prizes for work that should be considered kingdom-work — these are but a few of the worldly, pagan devices we employ. We court the big donors and shun the small. We use glamorous names to lure people to church and high-pressure sales techniques to get them to the altar.

Our appeals are fretted with dead clichés, which are meaningless to the non-Christian. We hone our tactical razors on soul-winning techniques when the keen edge of our concern for others has been dulled. Method is no substitute for relationship, nor memorized platitudes for a clear-cut understanding of the gospel. We gloat over statistics and use them to gain status with our fellows, forgetting that bringing the lost to the Saviour is actually a work of the Holy Spirit. We are, at best, tools to be placed in his hands.

Another real danger is that of confusing the content with the form and the form with the content. When some kind of technique appears to work we canonize it, assuming that if others fail to subscribe to this same method of worship, prayer, or soul-winning, they lack spiritual know-how.

For example, some groups have been successful in a certain kind of evangelism, like home evangelism or small-group evangelism, so they become obsessed with the idea that the only evangelism that means anything is their particular kind. Some of those who have been brought into a new prayer experience through conversational prayer may feel that this is the only kind of effective prayer. They may be bored at the average prayer meeting because they are secretly convinced that the Lord turns a deaf ear to any prayer that is not "conversational." So we get the feeling that if we use the prescribed pattern, if we go through the right formula, then and only then will God work.

This indicates a kind of cultic mentality which does not recognize that although we need external form, it can never be substituted for (a) sincerity of heart, (b) purity of life, (c) love for others, and (d) the ministry of the Holy Spirit.

The Holy Spirit has no use whatever for our techniques or formulas. He uses our warmth, sincerity, and love.

There is an inwardness to true religion. This is the beginning point. Our churches and denominations and organizations must have structure, but the structure itself is only a framework in which the content of faith and the dynamic of the Holy Spirit operate. To substitute one for the other is like separating the body from the spirit. To do this is to repeat the tragic mistake of Israel, who took the God-given patterns of worship, twisted them out of shape through idolatry, and squeezed out their meaning by relying too heavily on form and too little on content.

Structure we must have, but it can be no substitute for the vitality of Christian experience. It is only the Spirit of God who can bring true worship. It is only the Spirit of God who can bring religious forms to life and cause structure and symbol to speak to the hearts of men.

CONCLUSION

Hosea's message fits the pattern of revelation described in Hebrews 1:1-2: "In many and various ways God spoke of old to our fathers by the prophets; but in these last days he has spoken to us by a Son. . . ."

"In many and various ways" — Hosea illustrates the varied means by which the Lord spoke to his people. God's voice was heard in the events of history: armies marched, cities fell, kings were toppled from their thrones at his command. Confronted with the defection of princes and priests, he commandeered the talents and traits of Hosea and pressed them into service to put his Word across. Even tragedy became a channel of revelation, for through frustration and heartache Hosea learned to know the will and ways of God as few have. Gifted with extraordinary insight into the meaning of his people's past, he infused the covenant with new vitality when the vampires of idolatry, immorality, and injustice had almost sapped its life blood.

Hosea not only "spoke to the fathers" of his generation but he looked beyond them to the greater day of which the New Testament speaks. His message anticipates God's final Word in Christ. With great expectation he pictures a time when the kingdom of Israel, sawn asunder by Rehoboam's rashness and Jeroboam's ambition, will be reunited under One Head, as David their king leads them (1:11; 3:5).

No event in Israel's history after Hosea's times, not even the return from exile, has been grand enough in scope to fulfill this prophecy. Its fulfillment is found in Christ, David's Son, in whose kingdom — both present and coming — all Old Testament promises of hope come true. Although Paul's note about Israel's salvation (Romans 11:26) reminds us that God has included Israel in his future program, Peter's interpretation of Hosea's prophecies suggests that it is in the Church of Christ that the promises of Hosea seek their fulfillment:

> Once you were no people but now you are God's people; once you had not received mercy but now you have received mercy.
> (I Peter 2:10; cf. Hosea 2:3)

We must not miss the point here. God's promises to Israel will be fulfilled in the future experience of Israel and in the Church, the new people of God. This idea needs to be underscored because some are tempted to view our own country as the new land of the covenant, through whom God's program is being carried on in our age. That America is a land lavishly blessed by God, we cannot doubt. But the whole sweep of Biblical revelation insists that God entered into solemn and binding covenant with only one nation — Israel. In the Christian era his work is accomplished not by a nationality but by a Church comprised of some from almost every tribe and nation. The tasks of the kingdom are not dependent on the American way of life, as splendid as that may be, but on the obedience and dedication of the Church around the world, commissioned to make disciples of all nations.

All this is not to say that Hosea has no word for us as

a nation. He brings us as nations, and as individuals, face to face with some great Biblical realities which know no cultural, social, or national bounds, and can be ignored only to our great hurt.

He confronts us with the fact that depending on God is a life-or-death matter, which must show itself in justice and righteousness among men. He urges us to fix our expectations in God, who holds the helm of history in his hands. He pleads with us to spell out the meaning of God's grace in all our dealings with others.

Faith, hope, and love were Paul's summary of these crucial Biblical themes. Hosea said them and lived them first. And by his own commitment he called for ours:

> Whoever is wise, let him understand these things;
>   whoever is discerning, let him know them;
> for the ways of the Lord are right,
>   and the upright walk in them,
>   but transgressors stumble in them.
>
>   (14:9)

CHART OF KINGS AND PROPHETS
AT THE TIME OF HOSEA

KINGS OF JUDAH		PROPHETS		KINGS OF ISRAEL	
8th	Amaziah 800-783		A M O S	Jeroboam II	786-746
C E N T U R Y	Uzziah 783-742) I)) S)) A	H O S			
				Zechariah	746-745
				Shallum	745
	Jotham 742-735) I	)	E	Menahem	745-738
B.C.	Ahaz 735-715) A) H	)))	A	Pekahiah	738-737
		) M		Pekah	737-732
		) I		Hoshea	732-724
	Hezekiah 715-687)	) C) A) H		ISRAEL FALLS TO ASSYRIA 722/721	

INDEX TO BIBLICAL REFERENCES

113